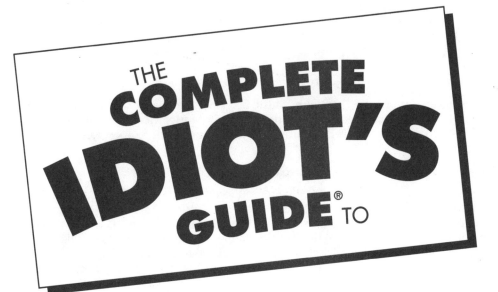

THE COMPLETE IDIOT'S GUIDE® TO

Playing the Guitar

Second Edition

by Frederick Noad

ALPHA

A Pearson Education Company

International Standard Book Number: 0-02-864244-9
Library of Congress Catalog Card Number: 2001093548

04 03 02   8 7 6 5 4 3 2

Interpretation of the printing code: the rightmost number of the first series of numbers is the year of the book's printing; the rightmost number of the second series of numbers is the number of the book's printing. For example, a printing code of 02-1 shows that the first printing occurred in 2002.

Printed in the United States of America

Note: This publication contains the opinions and ideas of its author. It is intended to provide helpful and informative material on the subject matter covered. It is sold with the understanding that the author and publisher are not engaged in rendering professional services in the book. If the reader requires personal assistance or advice, a competent professional should be consulted.

The author and publisher specifically disclaim any responsibility for any liability, loss, or risk, personal or otherwise, which is incurred as a consequence, directly or indirectly, of the use and application of any of the contents of this book.

Publisher
Marie Butler-Knight

Product Manager
Phil Kitchel

Managing Editor
Jennifer Chisholm

Senior Acquisitions Editor
Renee Wilmeth

Development Editors
Phil Kitchel
Amy Zavatto

Production Editor
Katherin Bidwell

Copy Editor
Laura Morelli

Portrait and Technical Illustrations
Linda Trujillo

Cartoons and Additional Illustrations
Chris Sabatino
Jody Schaeffer

Recording Engineer
Greg Steele of Derek Studios

Cover Designers
Mike Freeland
Kevin Spear

Book Designers
Scott Cook and Amy Adams of DesignLab

Indexer
Riofrancos & Co. Indexes

Layout/Proofreading
Angela Calvert

Contents at a Glance

Contents

Foreword

If you are a seasoned guitar enthusiast, you are bound to be familiar with the name Frederick Noad. His numerous publications, encompassing virtually every aspect of guitar playing, have become best-sellers, known throughout the world. If you have not heard of him, and you are about to venture into this book, you are embarking on a great journey of music and delight in learning to play the guitar.

It is no mean feat to write a guitar instruction book. The author has to possess a rare combination of gifts—namely, a thorough and total command of the instrument, a complete grasp of the guitar's history and repertoire, the ability to organize and impart information in logical, easily digestible steps, with the artistry of a master instructor. This paints a perfect portrait of Frederick Noad.

The book for which Mr. Noad is probably best known is *Solo Guitar Playing*. Through this publication and his many instructional television programs, he has introduced literally hundreds of thousands of people to the classical guitar. Many guitar teachers find that their students do not wish to limit themselves to learning just one style of playing. These students are equally fascinated by folk-picking styles, flamenco strums, blues licks, and classical etudes. It is for this broader-minded category of guitar student that Mr. Noad has written this book.

So—if you are a complete beginner, or if you have played for a while and are looking to broaden your style, or if you are an experienced teacher needing a versatile approach to meeting your students' demands, this is the book for you.

Starting with practical advice about how to choose your first guitar, the author leads you simply and thoroughly through each necessary step toward making your own music. As soon as you have learned how to hold your guitar, you will begin to play. By the time you are ready to read music, you will have achieved some basic expertise on your guitar and from there—well, the sky's the limit!

From this book, you will learn how to play melodies, chords, chordal accompaniments for songs, folk picks, 12-bar blues, rockabilly licks, flamenco, and some of the most beautiful pieces in the classical repertoire. Although this is an introductory book, Mr. Noad does much more than scratch the surface of each aspect he covers. He gives you a solid foundation from which you can choose the styles of guitar playing that you most enjoy.

In my experience, this is the best beginners' guitar book that I have encountered. As a professional guitar teacher for over 30 years, Frederick Noad's books have been my faithful traveling companions, and I am very pleased and gratified to have added this book to the forefront of my teaching library.

—Edward Flower

Edward Flower studied guitar with José Tomas in Alicante, Spain and has performed around the world with such chamber music groups as the Academy of St. Martin-in-the-Fields and the Chamber Music Society of Lincoln Center and such theater companies as the Royal Shakespeare Company and the Juilliard Theater. An accomplished composer/arranger, he was head of the Guitar Department at Ithaca College for 19 years. He has also taught at Bennington College, Boston University Tanglewood Institute, Colgate University, University of Connecticut, Simon's Rock College, and Wesleyan University.

He is featured on the following recording labels: Argo, EMI, Classic Editions, Musical Heritage Society, and Telarc. His most recent recording, *Chords & Thyme,* is with the Dorian label, for which the sheet music is published by Mel Bay Publications.

Introduction

The guitar is a wonderfully versatile instrument. It is portable, needs no accompanist because it provides harmony as well as melody, and has an intrinsically beautiful tone which is sensitive to human touch. The higher levels of solo playing take time and practice, as with any instrument, but the guitar can be a pleasure from the first day and the first successful sounding of a chord.

I have deliberately departed from conventional teaching methods in this book to try to give you a quick start at enjoyable music without too much theory. I have done this by relying on the help of the tablature system—an easy way to show where to place the fingers which avoids some of the trickier aspects of standard notation such as sharps and flats. This does not mean that these topics are bypassed. They're all there, but thanks to tablature you don't have to hold back from playing interesting pieces while you learn the fundamentals of music.

I have presented the material in a step-by-step approach, with each chapter building on the one before it. Ideally you will make steady forward progress, gradually increasing your knowledge and skill. However, human nature being what it is, many of you will jump ahead to try the more advanced pieces. If you are one these, bookmark where you left your step-by-step study so that you can come back to the same place and not fall into the trap of dipping aimlessly here and there.

A word on styles. This book teaches you how to read music and tablature, concentrating on the fingerstyle (as opposed to pick) guitar. Later you may decide that the electric guitar is your preference, and that you would like to play lead or backup with a group. This is obviously a different field, but what you have learned here about rhythm, harmony, and notation will speed your progress; in fact a basic knowledge of the original instrument is a great advantage.

For many of you, this is going to mean a whole change of life and a tremendous source of enjoyment. The study of the guitar is exciting because there is always something new to discover and achieve, and as long as you live there will always be more. For some it becomes a social activity through local guitar societies, with the chance to play duets or ensembles with other enthusiasts and perhaps perform for the group. For others it becomes like a meditation, a quiet hour after a day's work which lifts the mind gradually from the humdrum to the sublime.

Like the many other useful volumes in this series, this book is written with the absolute beginner in mind. You are not expected to know anything about music in general or the guitar in particular. However, chances are you have an interest in music and would like to explore the possibilities of the guitar in a way that is not too complicated. If so, this is the book for you. So now, to work and good luck.

How to Use This Book

It is best to proceed sequentially through the text. Each chapter builds on the one that came before. Some people may wish to race ahead to the more difficult pieces, but even if you have some guitar-playing experience already, it's best to review and make sure that you're doing everything right. Remember that bad habits, once learned, are very hard to undo!

Many of the techniques I'll be describing in this book were developed to teach players who wished to play in classical style. You may wonder why you should learn them if your taste runs in other directions: to folk, rock, or jazz. The fact is that a strong grounding in proper technique can help you play better no matter what style you eventually choose. There's a reason why all those classical guitarists over the years developed specific ways of holding the instrument, sitting, and playing. Why throw out centuries of knowledge?

The book will also teach you how to read guitar tablature. This system of notating guitar music is very simple and practical, and is used in all styles of guitar instructional books. Learning tablature will make it easy for you to learn new pieces in any style very quickly; it will also help you write down your favorite pieces, so you don't forget how to play them. With home computer programs such as Speedscore and others, it is now possible to produce complete tablature for any arrangement with ease.

To make it easier for you to use, I've divided this book into parts. They are:

Part One: Preparing to Play. This part tells you a little bit about the history of the guitar, the different types of guitars that are available to play, and helps you decide which is the best one for you. Once you get the instrument home, the first problem the beginning guitarist faces is getting, and staying, in tune. So, this part concludes with some basic information on stringing, setting up, and tuning your instrument.

Part Two: Getting Started. Here's where the excitement begins. You're ready to sit down with your guitar—but how do you hold it? It seems simple, but there are some good habits to develop from the start that will help you play more easily. And, once you've got it comfortably in position, you have to learn some basics of left- and right-hand technique. Here we start on both hands.

Part Three: Tunes and Tablature. This part introduces the wonderful world of tablature. Using tablature will enable you to learn quickly some new rhythms for the right hand, and some new fingering techniques for the left. These are also introduced in this section.

Part Four: Making Notes. After learning tablature, it's time for standard music notation. Not all books use guitar tablature, and it would be a shame to limit yourself to those that do. Also, learning notation will help you understand some basic elements of music theory, such as scales and chords. But don't worry—it's not too hard, and it can even be fulfilling and fun.

Part Five: Regional Styles. Good guitarists can play different types of music as the spirit moves them. This section demystifies the common styles and makes them easy to understand.

Part Six: Taking Off. Here's where all of your hours of practice pay off. You'll learn new chords and some great classical pieces, and you'll venture bravely where all guitarists long to go: up the fingerboard.

There are three Appendixes—one listing other books and videos for further study, a second listing guitarists you should know, and a final list of key terms that will aid in your learning.

In addition, I've included a couple of categories of information throughout the book that will help broaden your guitar education:

Take Note
Definitions of key words in the text.

Pick Hit
Facts, stories, and trivia about the guitar.

Key Thought
Helpful tips, plus advice for making the most of the information in the book.

Guitar Gods

Thumbnail biographies of well-known performers in all styles.

Acknowledgments

For major contributions to this book I should like to thank Ed Flower and Nellie W. Fink for their tremendous work and skill in the production of the CD that accompanies this book. In addition Ed had many helpful suggestions, and contributed a delightful solo to the Blues chapter as well as helping with many of the "teacher accompaniments" featured on the CD. Thanks also to Larry Sandberg for major work on the Blues and Rock and Roll chapters and Howard Heitmeyer in connection with the section on Latin Rhythms. Both generously shared their considerable expertise in these areas. Dr. Hiro Minamino kindly shared his views and made valuable suggestions. My particular thanks to Linda Trujillo for her wonderful portrait sketches and technical illustrations. Thanks also to Dave McCumisky, Rick Calderilla, and Jan Nelson for help in sorting through a mass of guitar methods and collections for the appendixes. Thanks to editor Richard Carlin for his considerable contribution, particularly in the areas of "Guitar Gods" and "Pick Hits." Finally, thanks to my wife, Marilyn, for going through the complete manuscript a number of times and offering valuable suggestions.

Part 1
Preparing to Play

What is this musical instrument called the guitar? Where did it come from? What types of music can be played on it? What different types of guitars are available, and what's the best instrument to buy? Before you even pluck a note, you're faced with all of these questions, and more. But don't worry. We'll be with you every step of the way. In this first part of the book, we'll answer all of these questions—and others—and then you'll be ready to play your first notes.

Chapter 1

The Guitar: A Noteworthy History

In this Chapter

➤ The ancient roots of the guitar

➤ Early guitar masters

➤ The growth of the classical style

➤ The guitar in America

➤ The folk revival

➤ The most popular instrument today

Before you begin to learn to play the guitar, you might be curious to learn a little bit about the instrument and where it came from. Although there have been stringed instruments around for centuries, the guitar in its present form is a relatively recent innovation—and the electric guitar has only really been with us since the 1950s.

Knowing about earlier guitarists and their styles of music will help you choose the kind of music you'd like to play. Thanks to recordings, we can hear today the music of sixteenth-century lutenists and then (at the flip of a CD) listen to twentieth-century heavy metal. All styles are open to us—we simply have to learn that they are available.

Our journey begins in ancient Egypt, where we will see that guitar-like instruments were already entertaining the Pharaohs...

The Ancient Roots of the Guitar

The guitar has a noble and ancient history. A plucked string instrument with the in-curving sides of the guitar is to be found on a tomb sculpture of the King of Thebes of the thirty-seventh century B.C., and a relief sculpture from Cappadocia of c. 1000 B.C. even shows an Egyptian guitar-like instrument with signs of frets. Evidence exists also of plucked instruments of extreme antiquity in Persia and Arabia.

Early Guitar Masters

In the Christian era, the guitar is mentioned in two forms in the thirteenth century: the Latin guitar and the Moorish guitar. Both are illustrated in beautiful miniatures in the manuscript "Cantigas de Santa Maria" attributed to Alfonso the Wise of Spain. Of the two, the Latin guitar is closer to the figure-eight shape of the guitar as it developed in Spain and Italy.

Take Note
Tablature is a special system of notation developed to show the positioning of the fingers on the fingerboard or neck. Guitar tablature has six lines, representing the six strings; the numbers on the lines show at which fret the finger should be placed to play the note.

In early sixteenth-century Spain, the *vihuela* became the instrument of choice for the serious musician. The vihuela was in fact an early form of the guitar, with six pairs of strings. Vihuela music may be played without alteration on the modern guitar. The only significant difference was the pairing of strings to produce a stronger sound, comparable to the 12-string guitar of today. The vihuela was played with the fingers, and a considerable repertoire of music existed for it in the notation form known as "tablature." The tuning was like that of the Renaissance lute, which in the rest of Europe was considered the "King of Instruments" and whose music is now a fertile source for guitarists.

At the same time, a smaller guitar, first with four and then with five sets of strings (known as courses), developed as a less sophisticated instrument for chording and the strumming style known as *rasgueado* used as accompaniment for the dance.

Surprisingly, at the end of the sixteenth century, the vihuela went out of favor and it was the humbler form of guitar that survived, now established with five courses. The name Spanish guitar became attached to this instrument, possibly to distinguish it from the earlier four-course variety, although guitars were also well known in Italy. Francesco Corbetta (c. 1615–1681), a famous Italian player, published extensively in the finger style that went beyond simple chording. Corbetta's playing was so popular that it soon became the rage among seventeenth-century courtiers in France and England, launching the guitar in those countries. In France the talented Robert de Visée (c. 1660–c. 1720) played frequently for Louis XIV, to whom he dedicated his collection of pieces published in 1682. Back in Spain, Gaspar Sanz's famous 1674 instruction book included detailed technique instruction and a fine collection of pieces that are still widely played.

The history of the guitar includes periods of fantastic popularity followed by periods of decline. The eighteenth century proved a time of low ebb for the guitar, until at its end the double strings gave place to single ones, and the sixth string was added to create the familiar form of today's guitar. Sheep's gut was used for the first three strings. The basses were formed by winding silver-plated copper wire onto a core of silk thread.

With the sixth string came a new wave of popularity with the public, led and inspired by virtuoso players who also composed and wrote instruction methods for the guitar in its new form. The main centers were Vienna and Paris, and great players such as Mauro Giuliani (1781–1829) from Italy and Fernando Sor (1778–1839) from Spain were drawn to emigrate to the north where enthusiastic audiences and students awaited them. Both composed extensively for the guitar, and laid the foundation for the solo repertoire. Ferdinando Carulli (1770–1841) produced a guitar method that is used to this day, and the "25 Melodious Studies" of Matteo Carcassi (1792–1853) are still part of the standard student repertoire.

Following this great wave of popularity came a period of decline and neglect, and by the middle of the nineteenth century the guitar was little played and rarely heard in concert. It was really thanks to Francisco Tárrega (1852–1909) that public interest was again awakened.

Although not as active a performer as Sor or Giuliani, Tárrega's reputation spread due to his wonderful compositions and his ability to produce an extremely beautiful and distinctive sound. This was due partially to his intimate knowledge of the guitar fingerboard and use of the higher positions on it to achieve a particular romantic quality. The general public tended to become familiar only with the first five frets or so of the guitar, and to favor student pieces that stayed within this limited range. Tárrega ignored these limitations to concentrate on works that exploited the whole guitar, and as a result founded a school of playing and composing that survives today.

Although not a student of Tárrega, Andrés Segovia (1893–1987) in a sense carried on the tradition and played Tárrega's works extensively in concert. Where Tárrega had been somewhat retiring as a player, and really preferred playing for intimate groups of friends and admirers, Segovia took the guitar to the world, and brought the world into his concerts with a hitherto unknown level of virtuosity and musicianship. It was due to him that the guitar is now recognized as an instrument worthy of serious study, and his interaction with composers inspired the bulk of the existing repertoire.

Guitar Gods

Andrés Segovia, one of the greatest musicians of the twentieth century, was born in Linares, Spain, on February 21, 1893. At the age of five he was taken to live with his uncle in Granada. His uncle encouraged him to learn the violin, but little Andrés was captivated by the sound of a guitar played by a local flamenco performer in his uncle's house. In the absence of formal training Segovia became, as he put it, "both teacher and pupil," a combination that produced the most celebrated guitarist of the twentieth century.

Segovia's sound was unique, and he literally captured the world with his sensitive and romantic concerts. He was concerned with the limitations of the guitar concert repertoire and launched a campaign to persuade prominent composers to write for the guitar, including Villa-Lobos, Castelnuovo-Tedesco, Rodrigo, and many others. His master classes in Siena, Italy, and in Santiago de Compostela, Spain, were a magnet to serious students, many of whom are leading players today.

It is because of Segovia that the classical guitar is well accepted today in music academies and universities. He gave the guitar stature, and the level of his personal musicianship forced critics to recognize in him a performer camparable to Fritz Kreisler or Pablo Casals. Segovia's genial nature brought him into contact with many famous people of his day, and as he said shortly before his death in 1987, "I have lived a long life, but a broad one."

In parallel with the growth of composed music for the guitar came popular developments in the field of folk music. In Spain the guitar had been used since the earliest times as a strummed accompaniment for dancing, and it had a long and respected history as an accompaniment for the voice. In the nineteenth century, the style known as flamenco evolved as accompaniment for the songs and dances of Andalusia. Inspired by the gypsies and deriving from their songs and dances as they blended with traditional folk music, the style developed into a complex and vigorous art form. The guitar was the principal instrument of accompaniment, and the continuing search for variety combined with a spirit of competition among the players resulted in an elevation of guitar technique to its highest levels. Many flamenco guitarists do not read music, and the style evolved primarily through exchange of ideas and experimentation. The legendary Ramón Montoya (1880–1949) is credited as the originator of many of the best *falsetas,* the name given to the musical phrases used to intersperse the verses of the songs and to embellish the dance accompaniments. Traditionally flamenco has not been considered as a solo art for the guitarist, the player being essentially a skilled accompanist for the song and dance. However today flamenco guitarists appear in concert and play improvisations based on their accompaniment skills to the delight of the fans or aficionados.

In the academic world of today the guitar has achieved a level of recognition and respect that was certainly lacking 50 years ago. Today many universities and music conservatories offer a music degree with the guitar accepted as the major instrument. In the popular field, the guitar holds its own in spite of the comparative ease of playing of the synthesizer. Though the sound is electronically amplified and often deliberately distorted, the human touch is always apparent, and no keyboard can ever quite simulate the effect of fingers on strings.

The Guitar in America

The acoustic guitar came to America in the 1850s, thanks mainly to immigrants from Eastern Europe. Guitar maker Christian Friedrich (C. F.) Martin left his native Germany because of dissatisfaction with the restrictive guilds that oversaw all instrument making back home. Meanwhile, factories were built to turn out inexpensive guitars by the dozens, and mail order catalogs like Sears Roebuck and Montgomery Ward began selling five-dollar instruments.

In the nineteenth century the guitar was promoted as a parlor instrument for young ladies to play. In the time before phonographs and radio, music-making was a favorite amateur activity. Young women were especially encouraged to learn music as an important social skill. While the piano was large and ungainly, the guitar was small and sweet-voiced; at the time, most guitars were far smaller than today's jumbo models, and they were all strung with gut strings in the classical style. Because of this, the guitar was thought to be an ideal instrument for young ladies, and it soon became popular.

As stage performers began taking up the guitar in the early twentieth century, they clamored for louder instruments that could fill a concert hall. Guitar makers responded by making bigger guitars; others began experimenting with different shapes for the guitar's body to improve bass response and volume. The Martin company made an important contribution in the teens with the introduction of their so-called D or Dreadnought guitar. With a wider lower bout (or half of the body), and with construction strong enough to withstand the newly introduced steel strings, the instrument was immediately popular for its loud bass volume and carrying power.

In the twenties and thirties, guitars began replacing banjos as the instrument of choice in jazz bands. Jazz players needed guitars that were louder still. The Gibson company introduced jumbo-sized instruments with carved tops and f-holes that were ideally suited to the new jazz music. Soloists like Eddie Lang helped popularize the guitar in jazz, although it took a French gypsy musician named Django Reinhardt to really show the jazz potential of the guitar.

Guitar Gods

Django Reinhardt was born in Luberchies, Belgium, on January 23, 1910, to gypsy parents. While young, Reinhardt suffered from an injury in a caravan fire, so that his left hand had only two functional fingers, making his lightning-fast speed that much more incredible! By 1922, he had settled in Paris, accompanying the singer Jean Sablon on popular standards. In the late twenties, he met violinist Stephane Grappelli, and the two formed the famous Quintet of the Hot Club of France, featuring three guitars, violin, and bass. Reinhardt played a Maccafieri guitar, made by the French Selmer Musical Instrument Company. It featured an unusual shape, including a wide, ovoid sound hole, and a large cutaway in the upper left corner of the body, to facilitate fingering up the neck. The quintet made many popular recordings through the thirties, until World War II led Grapelli to seek refuge in London. After the war, Reinhardt continued to play with various groups, including Duke Ellington, until his death in 1953.

The search for louder guitars led to some odd hybrids, including all-steel-bodied guitars with built-in, cone-shaped resonators. But it was the experiments of player Les Paul that led to the biggest innovation of them all: an electric guitar featuring a solid wood body. Instrument maker Leo Fender was quick to pick up on Paul's lead, introducing three solid-body models in the 1950s: the Broadcaster, the Telecaster, and the Stratocaster. The latter two instruments are still made today and remain favorites of rock players everywhere.

The Folk Revival

In the sixties, there was a veritable guitar renaissance, sparked by two different movements. One was the so-called "folk revival," in which young people with guitars performed topical songs of the day. Bob Dylan was the best known and probably the greatest of these singer/guitarists, and his songs influenced hundreds of others.

The second big influence was the arrival of the Beatles in America, and the British Invasion. When the Beatles first appeared, everyone copied their hair styles, clothing (down to their boots), and—naturally—musical instruments. The Rickenbacker guitar, favored by John Lennon, and the Hofner bass, played by Paul McCartney, were soon the most in-demand instruments in music stores across America. Instrument makers rushed to give the Beatles free instruments so that they could benefit from the publicity.

The British Invasion also spawned guitar gods like Eric Clapton, influenced by American blues players. A veritable war broke out among partisans of the Fender Stratocaster versus the equally popular Gibson Les Paul—some defended one as the "holy grail" of guitar sound, while others went for the other. Added "effects"—from wah-wah to fuzztone—were an additional arsenal in the guitar's acoustic army. One of the first guitarists to use these effects in a truly musical way was Jimi Hendrix, whose flamboyant stage presence only added to his popularity.

Take Note
Fuzztone is an artificial distortion sound that is added electronically by a special feature in a guitar's amplifier. The wah-wah pedal adds a crying sound.

Today the guitar is firmly ensconced as one of the most popular instruments among amateur musicians. Knock on somebody's front door, and you'll probably find a guitar in the house. It's easy to play, portable, and adaptable to just about any style of music.

The Least You Need to Know

➤ The guitar has been around a long time.

➤ Players in the Renaissance developed the classical, finger-style of playing the guitar.

➤ In America, the guitar became popular as a folk instrument.

➤ Electric guitars revolutionized the way the instrument was played.

➤ Today, you can play many styles of music on the guitar.

Chapter 2

What Is a Guitar?

In this Chapter

➤ The parts of the guitar

➤ Guitar styles: classical, flamenco, folk, jazz, and rock

➤ Guitar types: classical, acoustic, electric

➤ More guitar talk

➤ Selecting a guitar

➤ Guitar variants

Now that we know something of the instrument's past, let's learn more about the different types of guitars that are available to play. First, we'll take a guided tour of a typical guitar, so we learn how to talk about the various parts of the instrument, from *peg head* to *bridge*.

Once we've learned the guitar parts, we'll be ready to discuss the major differences between classical, folk, jazz, and electric/rock guitars. Why is choosing the right type of guitar so important? You can't play like Andrés Segovia if you choose Eddie van Halen's guitar, or vice versa.

Each type of guitar presents its special features and poses special challenges for the beginner. Getting the best guitar for the style of music you want to play is the goal here. You may even find that you'll want more than one instrument to suit your different musical personalities!

The Parts of the Guitar

Before discussing the types of guitars available, it's important to understand the common names for the various parts of the guitar. The accompanying diagram shows these parts clearly, along with names for the fingers of each hand.

A typical guitar and its parts

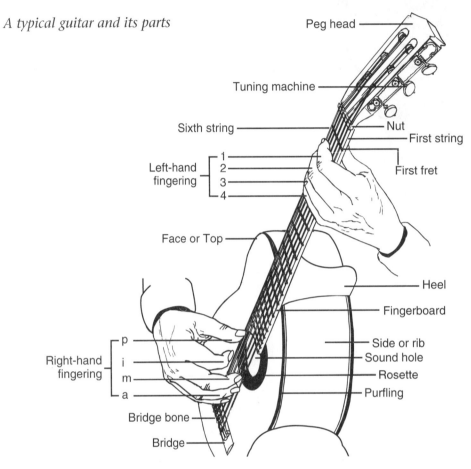

The *peg head* is found at the top of the neck of the guitar and holds the *tuning machines* or gears that are used to tune the strings. On classical guitars, this peg head is usually slotted; on acoustic, jazz, and rock guitars, it is usually solid. No matter—it performs the same function.

The *nut* is found at the bottom of the peg head and top of the guitar neck. It is made of bone and holds the strings in their proper position. The height of the nut also helps determine the string height or *action* of the guitar; classical players generally go for a higher action, while electric and jazz players like it lower.

Pick Hit
Guitars with sunburst finish (brighter toward the sound hole, darker toward the edges of the top) were first made to hide the fact that inferior wood was being used.

The neck of the guitar contains the *fingerboard.* Across the fingerboard run *frets*. By placing a finger against a fret, the player is able to raise the pitch of a string to play individual notes or chords.

The back of the neck, where it joins the body of the guitar, is called the *heel.* This may appear in a variety of shapes, and on very fancy guitars it may be carved with animals or human faces. It simply hides the joint between the neck and the guitar.

The front of the guitar is called the *face* or top. Around the edge of the face, there is usually *purfling* (often called *binding*) that hides the joint between the face and sides; similar binding appears around the back of the guitar. The face of the guitar usually features a round or oval *sound hole* (on acoustic instruments); sometimes f-shaped holes are used on jazz guitars. On some guitars, a fancy inlay called a *rosette* surrounds the sound hole for decorative purposes.

Guitar Gods

Charles Harden ("Buddy") Holley was born in Lubbock, Texas on September 7, 1936. He formed his first band while in high school, playing country-western music. A trip to Nashville in 1956 led to some early recordings, but they were not successful; the label misspelled his name as "Holly," which from that point became his performing name. Holly returned to Lubbock, where he listened carefully to another new artist, Elvis Presley, on record and radio. Holly revamped his band to play rock and roll. Holly was among the first to play a Fender Stratocaster, and he popularized it on his recordings and in TV and personal appearances. The twangy sound he achieved on his single-note lead work was very influential among rock players everywhere. Tragically, Holly died in a plane crash near Clear Lake, Iowa on February 2, 1959 during an ill-fated tour of the upper Midwest. His death is celebrated in the song "American Pie" as "the day the music died."

After the strings pass over the sound hole, they cross a slotted *bridge bone,* which directs the strings down to where they are fastened on the guitar's *bridge.*

While different types of guitars may have different features, these are the basic components you will find on most of them.

Guitar Styles

With so much variety it becomes necessary to look at the various types of guitar and to explore the best uses for each. Before going shopping it is obviously important to decide which style appeals to you the most, and which guitar will serve you best.

➤ Classical: If you're interested in playing classical music, you'll want to play a *Spanish* or *classical*-style guitar.

➤ Flamenco: For flamenco, a Spanish-made instrument is best.

➤ Folk/Traditional/Blues: For these styles, the standard *acoustic* guitar is the best choice, although some folk players prefer the softer sound of the Spanish classical guitar.

➤ Jazz: You can play either an acoustic or electric instrument, although many jazz players prefer a special, large-bodied hybrid instrument called a *hollow-body electric.*

➤ Rock: An *electric* guitar is mandatory for the hard-rockin' player.

More Guitar Talk

Some other terms you might hear when people are discussing different types of guitars are:

➤ Fan Bracing: This is a style of internal construction commonly used on Spanish guitars. It is considered essential to the production of fine tone, and patterns very slightly from one maker to another.

Pick Hit
Fan Bracing is so-called because the pattern of braces resembles an open fan.

➤ X-Bracing: This is the style of bracing commonly used on today's acoustic guitars. It is designed to withstand the high tension of steel strings.

➤ Arch Top: This refers to a curved or arched (as opposed to flat) top. Arched top instruments are said to have a warmer sound, like a violin.

➤ Solid Body: This is a type of construction in which the body of the instrument is a solid piece of wood, fiberglass, or other material. The body of the instrument has no acoustic resonance, so that, without amplification, the instrument produces only a thin, barely audible sound. Hollow-body instruments have a sound chamber (like an empty box) which amplifies the sound.

Pick Hit
Guitarist Mason Williams had a No. 1 pop hit in 1968 with the instrumental "Classical Gas," featuring his solo classical guitar playing accompanied by full orchestra.

Selecting a Guitar

This is the type of guitar that developed from the earliest forms of four- and five-stringed instruments, reaching its final form in the early nineteenth century. In addition to being the type of guitar used for the solo "classical" repertoire, the Spanish or classical guitar is used for the accompaniment of folk songs, for the songs and dances of Latin America, and for the flamenco music of Spain. Throughout Europe it has long been the favorite accompaniment instrument for love songs and serenades.

The nylon-strung Spanish or classical guitar.

Traditionally the sides and back of a flamenco guitar differ in that they're made of cypress wood, which is distinguishable by its yellow color and lighter weight, but this is not always the case today because some of the great flamenco players prefer hardwood.

Classical guitars usually have a slotted peg head and are strung with nylon strings. Generally they are smaller than acoustic or electric instruments. The neck width is greater than on acoustic or electric guitars to facilitate the intricate left-hand work demanded in classical compositions.

Although the term "acoustic" really applies to any non-amplified guitar, it is commonly used to describe the steel-strung guitar used in country, folk, and blues styles. The steel strings give more volume than nylon, and also have a "brassier" sound.

Acoustic guitar players can play with their fingers (as do classical players), sometimes adding metal thumb and fingerpicks to enhance their sound. Others strum across all the strings—or play complex melody lines—using a flatpick (also called a *plectrum*).

The acoustic guitar has a beautiful rich sound in the hands of players like James Taylor, John Renbourne, Leo Kottke, and many others. It works well as an accompaniment instrument, and the best players also use it for solos and improvisations. However, for intricate solo work it is somewhat harder to play than the Spanish guitar.

Take Note
The thumbpick is a soft metal ring that fits over the thumb with a projection to the side that serves as a pick. Sometimes fingerpicks are also used for the fingers. The pick area projects beyond the end of the finger like a false nail. A flatpick is a thin, triangle-shaped piece of plastic, held between the thumb and first finger, that is used to strum across the strings or to pick individual notes.

The acoustic guitar

The jazz guitar

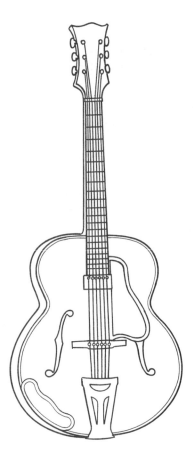

This type of guitar is normally played with a plectrum, and represents a transition from acoustic to electric guitar, because the guitar itself has some acoustic property although nowadays it is normally amplified. Although a component of the rhythm section of early jazz groups where its distinctive "chunk" sound would cut through and be heard without amplification, this guitar was also used extensively for melody and solo work, an example being the work of great players such as Django Reinhardt.

Distinguishing features include the violin-like f-holes which replace the circular sound hole of the traditional guitar. Often jazz guitars are larger in size than classical or acoustic guitars, and they usually have arched tops and backs, like a violin. This is said to improve their sound projection. Pickups are now built into the guitar, as are volume and tone controls.

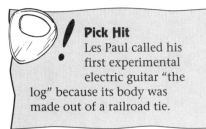

Pick Hit
Les Paul called his first experimental electric guitar "the log" because its body was made out of a railroad tie.

The pioneering guitarist Les Paul was a technical as well as musical wizard. He is famous for multitrack recorded performances, and his developments on the instrument itself led to the extensive use of solid-body guitars with no innate acoustic resonance. Used for chords and lead in contemporary rock groups, the solid-body guitar has no sound until it is plugged into an amplifier. The electronic sound from pickups is processed in inventive ways for special effects, including deliberate distortion. The result is a new creation that has a fingerboard and strings but acoustically shares little with the traditional guitar.

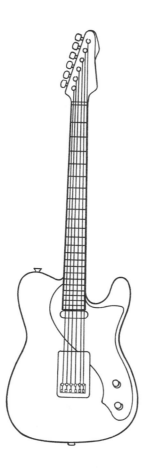

The solid-body electric guitar

Guitar Variants

While most of you will choose from among the four major types of guitars we've already described, there are some other noteworthy types of guitars that have been or are available.

➤ Bass Guitars. Perhaps the most popular guitar variant is not really a guitar at all—it is an electrified version of a standup bass, designed to be held like a guitar. Introduced in the fifties by Fender, the electric bass has become a standard component of all rock bands. It is tuned and played like a standard acoustic bass—so it's really a member of the violin family. Recently, acoustic guitar makers have designed acoustic bass guitars that are held like an electric bass but are intended for playing softer music.

➤ Smaller Instruments. Three-quarter-sized or half-sized guitars are made, often for children. The Martin Guitar Company recently introduced a specially sized guitar designed for women players, who tend to have smaller hands than men.

➤ Acoustic-Electric Guitars. This simply describes an acoustic guitar with built-in electric pickups, designed to be played through an amplification system. These are particularly attractive to people who like to play folk-style music, but the instrument needs to be heard in a club setting.

➤ 12-String Guitars. These large-bodied, double-strung guitars were much favored by blues players because of their loud volume. The strings were tuned an octave apart, giving the instrument a booming bass sound.

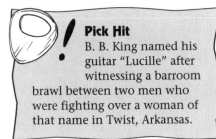

Pick Hit
B. B. King named his guitar "Lucille" after witnessing a barroom brawl between two men who were fighting over a woman of that name in Twist, Arkansas.

➤ Guitar Synthesizers. These instruments enable guitarists to enjoy the wide world of sounds available through synthesizers. They feature guitar-like construction and are held and played like a guitar, but actually they contain or connect to a synthesizer, which creates a variety of sounds.

There are also a wide variety of other guitar types—from tenor guitars to harp guitars—that were popular at one time or another, although they are rarely played or heard today.

The Least You Need to Know

➤ There are four basic types of guitar availables: Spanish/classical, Acoustic, Jazz, Electric.

➤ The Spanish guitar is strung with nylon strings, is moderate in size and soft in tone, and is best suited to classical, flamenco, and Latin folk styles.

➤ The acoustic guitar is larger, suited to folk and blues, and is strung with metal strings; it may be played with a flatpick or metal fingerpicks.

➤ The jazz guitar is larger still, often features built-in amplification, and is suited to single-note playing or chording in the jazz style.

➤ The electric guitar has a solid body, so it can only be played through an amplifier; it is suited to single-note or chord playing in the rock style.

➤ The type of guitar you buy will be determined to a large extent by what you want to play.

Chapter 3

Buying a Guitar

In this Chapter

➤ Before shopping

➤ Tips and pointers for choosing a guitar

➤ Fitting an instrument to you

➤ Common guitar brands

➤ Mail order

➤ Accessories

Buying a guitar can be an intimidating experience, particularly if you aren't yet a proficient player. How can you choose the right instrument if you can't even play it? But, the fact of the matter is there are some practical techniques you can use in selecting and buying an affordable instrument.

This chapter outlines some basic buying strategies that will work for you. These include pre-shopping tips: distinguishing among different types of guitars (drawing on the information from Chapter 2), fitting an instrument to your body type (and style of music), a brief overview of the common guitar brands, and whether to buy from a local music shop or by mail order.

Even if you could afford to own Eric Clapton's Stratocaster—and generally speaking you should buy the best guitar you can afford—you may have to be practical. This means buying a guitar . . . that won't empty your savings account. This chapter shows you how.

Before Shopping

As with all major purchases, it is important to do as much research as possible beforehand. Sources of information will be other players, teachers (local colleges may have a guitar program), and for those with access to the Internet a host of manufacturers' advertisements.

There are also guitar newsgroups on the Internet, which offer the opportunity to read the experiences of others and to ask for opinions.

Remember from Chapter 2 that there are several types of guitars made to play different styles of music. Before shopping, listen to different players and determine what kind of instrument you would like to play. While you may be able to learn on any instrument, it is better to select one that closely approximates the style you want to learn.

How Much to Spend

It may be wiser to borrow or rent an instrument for the first few months, until you determine your level of commitment to playing. On the other hand, an old, battered, poorly constructed instrument may be so difficult to play that you'll be discouraged from learning.

It's a good rule of thumb to purchase the most guitar you can afford. Generally, guitars hold their resale value—some in fact grow in value over the years. Buying a very cheap guitar may be self-defeating, because it may not suit your playing style or be so poorly made that it is difficult to play.

Acoustic vs. Electric

Many young players start out on an acoustic instrument because they can't afford a good-quality electric instrument and amplifier—or their parents can't stand the noise made by a beginning electric guitarist! Learning on an acoustic instrument will probably be a good experience for most players, even those who only aspire to playing speed-metal. But remember that the two instruments are quite different, and that you'll need to master a new set of techniques once you start playing an electric.

New vs. Used

A good used guitar can be an excellent value. Many people buy instruments and then discover that they simply lack the time or capability to play them. You can sometimes pick up a real bargain by scanning the local want-ads.

Here's a checklist for evaluating a used guitar:

1. Make sure the tuning machines all work and turn easily.
2. Check the body for cracks. Any crack, no matter how small, is a bad sign.
3. Check the neck for warping. Press a string down at each end of the fingerboard. It should touch all the frets.
4. Try playing a few notes and chords; see if the guitar responds easily.
5. Ask the owner if he/she is the original owner. Determine if the instrument has ever been repaired.

Shopping Tips

Once you determine what kind of guitar you want to buy, the next thing you need to do is determine how much guitar you can afford.

Many guitars are made in the Far East today, and there's nothing wrong with their craftsmanship. New American-made guitars tend to be more expensive, so most beginners are going to end up with an imported one. Luckily, the Asian makers make reasonably good guitars in all the popular styles, but obviously if your main interest is the classical/Spanish style, you should look for Spanish imports as well.

Guitar Gods

Lester Polfus was born in Waukesha, Wisconsin, on June 9, 1915. He began playing guitar as a youngster on local radio stations and at parties, taking various performing names. Eventually he settled on Les Paul as his pseud-onym, and worked as an accompanist with various popular singers from Bing Crosby to the Andrews Sisters. In the early forties, he began experimenting with a solid-body, electrified guitar; the result was the famous Gibson Les Paul model, introduced in the early fifties. Along with his wife Mary Ford, Paul made a series of highly influential and innovative recordings from the late forties to the early sixties. A pioneer in multiple-tracking, he added layer and layer of guitars and voices to make a veritable orchestra of Fords and Pauls. In the eighties and nineties, Paul has been coaxed out of retirement to perform as a jazz guitarist.

Sound Advice

To save money, inexpensive guitars are usually made of lesser-quality woods. You will rarely find an inexpensive instrument made of solid wood. Instead, *laminates* (a fancy name for plywood) are used. The appearance will be good, because quality woods are used to for the outer layer, and these guitars are very sturdy and unlikely to crack; but the sound of a plywood guitar is rarely as resonant as one made with solid woods. Sometimes the top, or soundboard, will be solid with laminated wood for the sides and back, which is preferable to plywood throughout.

The best classical guitars have sides and back of Brazilian or East Indian rosewood. The tops are of spruce or Canadian cedar with even spacing between the anular lines of the grain. The neck is usually made of Spanish or Honduras cedar, and the fingerboard of ebony. Folk or acoustic guitars can be made of spruce, maple, rosewood, or mahogany, each having a different characteristic sound. Folk guitars also use ebony fretboards, although cheaper instruments may use a plastic substitute. As well as costing more, the solid wood guitar will need more care since it is more susceptible to changes in temperature and humidity. Excessive dryness is a particular enemy of guitars.

At the very minimum, if you are playing an acoustic guitar, try to get a guitar with a solid wood face or top. This will give you the advantage of improved sound. The laminate body, meanwhile, will be better for you as a beginner because it is sturdier—less likely to crack or scratch with mishandling—and overall has less effect on the instrument's performance.

For electric guitars, it doesn't much matter what is used to make the body. In fact, the ideal is to have a strong, nonresonant body—the opposite of what you'd like in an acoustic instrument. Plywood, plastic, fiberglass—anything strong can be used. The body is more important for its decorative value—i.e., how it looks on stage—than its composition.

Fitting an Instrument to You

Besides choosing the type of instrument suited to the kind of music you'd like to play, it's important that the guitar you choose is one that you are comfortable playing. It's no good getting a super-deluxe, large-bodied jazz guitar if you are slightly built—no matter how (theoretically) good the instrument might be, *you* won't be comfortable playing it.

Common Guitar Brands

Guitar makers come and go but there are a couple of name brands that have been around for many decades that are known for the general quality of their instruments. Here's a partial listing, with some comments about them.

Japanese/Asian Makers

➤ Yamaha: This Japanese maker is well known for the quality of its beginner's instruments. They make a wide variety of styles of acoustic and electric guitars, most of which are copies of popular American models, although a few are original in design to Yamaha. They also make a line of classical-style guitars based on Spanish models.

➤ Alvarez-Yairi. This is another Japanese maker that makes a slightly glitzier guitar than Yamaha, with lots of "mother-of-pearl" (actually plastic) inlays. They are known primarily for acoustic, folk-styled guitars.

Guitar Gods

Little is known about the life of Robert Johnson, perhaps the most famous, and certainly most influential, of all the Delta blues guitarists. Born around the turn of the century, Johnson appeared at local parties and small gin joints by the early twenties, where older musicians like Son House heard him play and scoffed at his lack of abilities. Then, he disappeared for a few months. When he returned, House was astounded by the new talent Johnson showed on the instrument. Johnson is said to have "made a deal with the Devil," picking up his extraordinary skills by selling his soul. He tells the story of his encounter with Satan in his most famous composition, "Crossroads Blues." True to his rough-and-tumble life, Johnson made only a handful of recordings in the late thirties before a jealous girlfriend gave him a drink of poisoned liquor.

➤ Washburn: Originally, Washburn guitars were made by the Lyon & Healey Company in the late nineteenth and early twentieth centuries. The name was revived in the 1970s by a U.S. importer of Japanese guitars. They make a reasonably good line of acoustic, folk-styled guitars, as well as electric instruments.

➤ Takamine: A Japanese company specializing in copies of Martin guitars. Very playable and reasonably priced, they are good alternatives for those who want a Martin-style instrument. They also make classical guitars, including some fine handcrafted models under the Hirade brand name.

➤ Ibañez: They are best-known for their reasonably priced copies of popular electric guitars, including models inspired by Les Paul and the Stratocaster.

American Makers

➤ Guild: This venerable American maker was founded in the late forties to make jazz-style guitars, but they are best-known for their folk, acoustic instruments of the sixties. Not quite as celebrated as Gibson or Martin, Guild nevertheless makes dependable and playable instruments.

➤ Gibson: The Gibson Company has a long history, going back to the 1890s. After a period of corporate ownership in the 1970s, the company underwent a remarkable revival. Gibson makes acoustic, folk guitars; arch-top jazz models; and the famous Les Paul electric guitar (as well as other electric styles, such as the Flying V). Gibson has imported less expensive Japanese-made instruments that it has marketed under the Epiphone name.

➤ Martin: Founded in 1833, this company still makes its guitars in Nazareth, Pennsylvania. Martin makes some classical and acoustic-electric instruments, but basically is known for their large-bodied, Dreadnought (or "D") styled guitars. The gold standard for acoustic players.

➤ Fender: Founded in the early fifties by Leo Fender, this company is famed for two guitars, the Telecaster and Stratocaster, as well as its Jazzmaster bass. Like Gibson, the quality of its instruments declined during a period of corporate ownership from the middle sixties through the late seventies, but has recently come back. Original Stratocasters from the fifties are worth huge sums of money.

➤ Ovation: Perhaps the most radical of all new guitar designs came from the Ovation company in the early seventies. Acoustic guitarists either love them or hate them. These guitars have fiberglass bodies with a bowl-shaped back, although the soundboard or face is made of wood. The sound hole design is also eccentric, often featuring (depending on the model) several small holes in the upper left-hand bout of the instrument.

Spanish Makers

➤ Alhambra: Good-quality guitars from the province of Valencia, long a center of classical and flamenco guitars.

➤ Córdoba: In spite of the name, these traditional Spanish guitars also come from Valencia.

What Will a Dealer Do for You?

Remember that when you buy an instrument from a guitar store, you're giving them your business—so they should treat you like a valued customer! This should start even when you're "just looking." Here's a checklist of things to ask of your dealer:

➤ Will he play and demonstrate different instruments for you?

➤ Will he tune and adjust the guitar to your liking?

➤ Does he provide any free extras—a carrying case, extra strings, etc.—with your purchase?

➤ Does he offer repair services or additional warranties?

➤ Does he have a return/refund policy?

➤ Will he accept the instrument in trade if you decide to "upgrade" to something better?

Mail Order

At one time, most towns had a music store with a good selection of guitars on hand. Nowadays you may have to travel miles to find a well-stocked outlet. There are, however, several mail order dealers that specialize in guitars, often at discounted prices.

Here are some things to keep in mind when dealing with mail order:

➤ Make sure you've played the instrument—in a local music shop or at a friend's house—before ordering one.

➤ Make sure you have a reasonable "trial" period during which you can return the instrument for a refund (not just a credit).

➤ Pay for a reputable shipping service such as UPS or Federal Express, and insure the shipment.

➤ Determine who handles warranty repairs and adjustments.

➤ Examine the instrument carefully for damage when you receive it.

Accessories

When buying a new guitar, you should always get a good, sturdy case. Generally, there are three types of cases available:

➤ Chipboard: The cheapest, and least protective of your investment.

➤ Gig Bag: A lined bag made of vinyl or some plastic material that gives limited protection to your guitar.

➤ Hardshell Case: The heaviest and most durable protection you can get.

Obviously, you should go for the most protection you can afford. But never *ever* store or carry a guitar outside of its case, even if it's just a cardboard one. A case will help protect a guitar from bumps and scratches, and also can protect it against excessive humidity, sunlight, or heat, as well as other less-than-favorable conditions.

Other accessories you might consider are electronic tuners, extra sets of strings, straps, and guitar instruction books and videos. All of these items can be useful, although you don't need to buy them all at once. We'll be discussing some of these items in more depth in future chapters.

The Least You Need to Know

➤ Buying a guitar takes time and study.

➤ Be sure to get an instrument that suits your playing style and is easy for you to play.

➤ Shop carefully among new and used instruments, as well as local dealers and mail-order suppliers.

➤ Be sure to get a case to protect your investment.

➤ You can play *all* the music in this book on a Spanish-style nylon string guitar.

Chapter 4

Strings and Things

In this Chapter

➤ Setting the right "action" for your instrument

➤ Changing strings

➤ Choosing the right type of string

➤ Tuning

The strings form the key interface between you and your guitar. If you've never played a stringed instrument before, it may even feel uncomfortable for a while. But with the right playing action, your guitar will soon become easier to handle.

This chapter introduces you to some easy solutions for the trials and tribulations of playing a stringed instrument. It tells you what you need to know to make playing fun and easy from the beginning, and introduces the many options available to you among different types of guitar strings. And it will making tuning your guitar easier.

About the Fingers

The first thing a new guitarist notices is that the tips of the left-hand fingers can feel sore after a stretch of playing. This is particularly true if you're playing a steel-strung guitar, but is noticeable even with nylon strings.

Just as a trumpeter must develop his "chops," the guitarist will develop calluses. It may take several weeks—or even months—for these to develop. And, if you take a break from practicing, you may lose the calluses you've built up.

The Playing Action

For beginners, it is important not to have strings that are too high off the fingerboard, because this increases the necessary pressure for the left-hand fingertips to hold down a clear note or chord.

Guitar Gods

Riley B. King was born near the small plantation town of Itta Bene, Mississippi, on September 16, 1925. Like many other Delta blues players, he began his career as a sharecropper, playing guitar on the side. He emigrated to the Memphis area by the late forties, where he landed his own radio show. He took on the nickname of "Blues Boy," which was further shortened to B. B. In the early fifties, he recorded for the small RPM label, scoring a hit with "Three O'Clock Blues," followed by many others. His eloquent single-note solos were influenced by jazz guitarists like Lonnie Johnson and T. Bone Walker. In the middle sixties, rock guitarists like Eric Clapton began promoting King and his music, and he found an entirely new, young, white audience. King and his guitar, nicknamed Lucille, continue to perform hundreds of shows a year.

The strings are supported by detachable bones at the nut and bridge (see illustration). The nut bone, which is slightly grooved to provide a guide for each string, sets the height above the fingerboard at that end. If the strings are too low they will buzz against the frets. If they are too high, the guitar becomes hard to play, which can completely discourage you from continuing.

If the setting is too high, the nut bone needs to be removed and filed down from the underside. If it is too low, a sliver of cardboard or similar material may be inserted underneath, but this should be a temporary solution until a new bone of the right height can be obtained. On a classical guitar the height of the strings at the first fret will be about 1/16 in (1.5 mm).

At the bridge end, a similar adjustment can be made to the bridge bone to produce a height at the twelfth fret of approximately 3/16 in (5 mm). The reason the measurements are approximate is that the exact amount depends on the height of the frets and the total string length, both of which vary from maker to maker.

Note that these measurements are for the nylon string guitar. The metal strings of the acoustic guitar are set lower due to the greater tension, and for the sake of the left hand, steel strings need to be as low as is practical, consistent with clear sound.

Strings

Changing Strings

When you buy your guitar, chances are that it is correctly strung, and you will be able to see by looking at the bridge how the knot is tied. The illustration below shows the correct way to attach nylon strings to the bridge for the classical or Spanish guitar. After looping in the manner shown, the end should be trimmed so as to be clear of the soundboard. Otherwise it could cause buzzing.

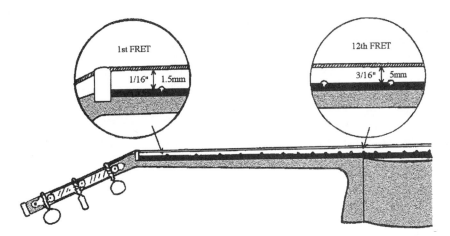

Approximate settings for comfortable playing action

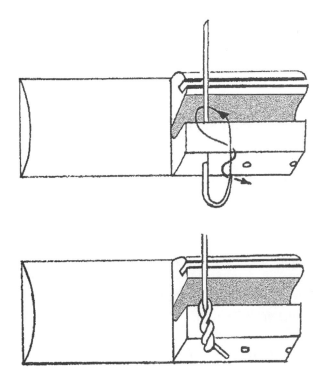

How the strings attach to the bridge

For acoustic or folk guitars, there is often an arrangement of six pegs in the lower part of the bridge. The string is simply looped around the peg and then the peg inserted into its hole to hold it fast.

Electric guitars feature an attachment at the end of the bridge, usually with six small pins. The loops of the strings are attached around these pins to be held securely. Jazz guitars often have a raised tailpiece and have their own unique method of string attachment.

> ### Guitar Gods
>
> Julian Bream, one of the greatest classical guitarists the world has known, was born in London on July 15, 1933. His interests range from early music—he plays the lute as well—to the music of today, including an affection for the jazz guitar of Django Reinhardt. As an early musician, Bream has revived music that lay dormant for centuries, and at the same time he has done more than anyone to widen the contemporary guitar repertoire by inspiring and commissioning works from major modern composers including Benjamin Britten, William Walton, Lennox Berkeley, and many others. Bream is a profound and dynamic interpreter, drawing repertoire from all possible sources and putting his totally original stamp on the music he performs.

At the peg-head end of the classical guitar, the string should be passed through the hole in the white bone barrel. Then pass the string back to make a loop around itself. Finally, holding the string by the end, turn the tuning key so that the twist you have made winds over the top of the barrel and away from you.

Acoustic folk guitars and electric models usually feature solid peg heads with large, steel-barrelled tuning machines. As with the classical guitar, the string is passed through a hole in the top of the barrel, and then the peg is simply turned to increase its tension. Excess strings should be cut off to avoid tangling in the tuning key and to keep a generally clean appearance.

Choosing Strings

Just as there are different types of guitars, there are different types of strings. Here are the principal types:

➤ Nylon strings are used on classical guitars. In fact, it is dangerous to use heavier strings on a classical guitar, because the instrument is not designed to withstand the high tension they produce. The three lowest strings are made of silver-plated copper wire wound on a core of nylon strands. The upper three are pure nylon filaments.

➤ Steel strings are designed for acoustic folk guitars. The bass strings are wound on a core of silk or nylon.

➤ Heavier wound metal strings are designed for electric guitars.

Core and winding materials vary among string makers, and you may wish to experiment with different types to see which produces the sound you like best.

Strings are also available with different shapes or contours, from flat to fully rounded. Strings are also sold in light, medium, or heavy gauges. This has to do with the amount of elasticity in the string: light-gauge strings are more elastic and therefore easier to play than heavy ones. Again, depending on the kind of music you play and your own personal taste, you'll be able to choose the proper string for you. It's always worthwhile to try different types of strings on your instrument to see if a simple change of strings can lead to improved sound and playability.

Raising the Dead

Strings have a natural life cycle. As they are exposed to air and the oils from your fingers, they tend to lose their elasticity and eventually their ability to sound cleanly. You can forestall this process by wiping the strings clean with a soft, dry cloth after you play. Dead strings may be revived temporarily by scrubbing with soap and water.

String Brands

Every player seems to have his or her own favorite "brand" of string. Unlike guitar brands, it's hard to make general statements about strings. While some guitar companies have their own name-brand strings, most do not make strings themselves but buy them from an established maker and repackage them. A reputable dealer or teacher should be able to recommend a good string for you. Remember also that different makers use slightly different terminology when referring to nylon, composite, or steel strings.

Tuning

To tune your guitar, you need a pitch reference. A tuning fork or pitch pipe can be used as a reference. If you buy a tuning fork (the more accurate pitch), be sure it is an E fork—not A, which is the more common type. The E note will give you the pitch for your first string.

Tuning to the Piano

Another good way to tune is by using a piano. If your piano is in tune, you can simply play each note and quickly tune the corresponding string.

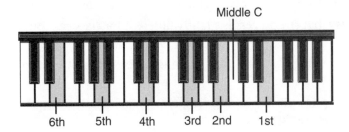

Tuning to the piano

Relative Tuning

With your first string in tune, it is possible to tune the rest of the guitar string by string. Here's how:

➤ Put a left-hand finger just behind the fifth fret of the second string and sound the string with any right-hand finger. It should sound the same as the first string open (i.e., with no frets used). If it doesn't, tighten or loosen it until it does.

➤ With the top two strings now in tune, put a finger behind the *fourth* fret of the third string. When you play it should sound the same as the second string. If it doesn't, tighten or loosen as above.

➤ With the top three strings in tune, place a finger behind the fifth fret of the fourth string. Adjust it to sound like the third string.

➤ With the top four strings in tune, place a finger behind the fifth fret of the fifth string, and align it to the fourth string.

➤ Finally, place a finger behind the fifth fret of the bottom string and tune it to the fifth string. That's all there is to it.

Tuning seems tricky at first but it comes with practice. In general don't be too delicate in turning the tuning keys—a very small increment won't make any difference. Sometimes it is easier to off-tune by an easily audible amount and then come back.

Electronic Tuning

Tuning can also be made almost foolproof with electronic tuning machines, in which either a meter or colored lights tell you when you're in tune. The cost of these is naturally higher than that of tuning forks or pitch pipes, but they are accurate and easy. The best kind allow you to play a note and then watch a needle that shows whether you're sharp or flat.

String Stretch

After putting on a new string, there is a tendency to believe that the string is slipping, because the pitch will drop slightly over a period of time after being tuned up. Actually this is the string stretching, and until the settling point is reached it will be necessary to tighten the string periodically. Professional players hasten this process by taking hold of the string and twisting it to get the stretch out.

The Least You Need to Know

➤ The action (or height) of the strings on your guitar is crucial to making it playable.

➤ Changing strings is easy, but the process is slightly different for classical, folk, and electric guitars.

➤ Buying the right type of strings for your instrument is important to maximize sound and playability.

➤ Tune your guitar with a pitch pipe or tuning fork, on a piano, relatively on the instrument itself, or with an electronic tuner.

Part 2
Getting Started

Now we're ready to play. First, we'll establish a good playing position and find some chords with the left hand. In Chapter 6 we'll bring in some right-hand variety, and after practicing this with a song we'll move on to learning about broken chords, known as arpeggios.

Beginning to Play

Besides learning the most comfortable and practical way to hold the instrument, this chapter will introduce us to some basic left-hand techniques. You will learn the simple chords that are used to accompany many popular songs, and also how to make quick and easy transitions between them.

These are the first steps in becoming a guitarist. And, like all steps, we will break it down so you can't possibly make a mistake.

Playing Position

Now that you're ready to play the guitar, it's important to learn how to hold it in a comfortable way. As you might expect, the different styles of playing have slightly different rules when it comes to handling the instrument.

A comfortable playing position is important to provide access to all parts of the guitar without strain. Classical players place the guitar on the left leg raised by a footstool so that the upper part of the leg will support the guitar without it slipping down. The sketch of Andrés Segovia shows the position favored by most professional players. Some performers have both feet flat on the floor and use a special type of cushion to raise and support the guitar, but this is less common.

The classical position

Most non-classical players support the guitar on the right leg. Traditionally flamenco players position the guitar at its widest point on the right leg. Most other styles use an informal position resting the guitar on the right leg. Some players use a cross-legged position, but there are physical disadvantages to this, notably the concomitant decrease in blood circulation.

Playing in a standing position, as in stage performance, requires a strap for support. The strap is attached at the bottom of the guitar's body to a pin and commonly attached at the top by a string tied around the bottom of the headstock, above the nut. Pins can be added to a guitar for this purpose, but this should be done by a professional repair technician.

This sketch of Ramón Montoya, considered the greatest flamenco player of his day, illustrates the traditional flamenco position.

Sitting Correctly

First, sit comfortably in an upright chair as illustrated above. I recommend using the classical position, with the left foot raised on a footstool or other support, because this provides the easiest access to all parts of the guitar. The height of the footstool will vary according to your height, but for most people four to six inches is enough to provide good support. Adjustable folding footstools are widely available at music stores at moderate cost and are the most convenient solution. However, in the early stages anything that raises and supports the foot will do.

To look at your hands, lean forward rather than pulling the guitar back. It is important to keep the guitar upright. As you look to your left at the tuning machines, keep them about the level of your shoulder; the axis of the guitar should not become too vertical.

The informal right-leg position. The sketch shows the position favored by the versatile Laurindo Almeida, a master of both classical and Latin American styles.

The Left Hand

At first we'll concentrate on the left hand. To play the chords, simply sweep the pad of the thumb across the strings—we'll add sophistication later.

The illustration shows the basic position of the left hand. Notice that the thumb is behind the neck, approximately behind the fret played by the first finger. Here is an excellent first exercise to establish and strengthen the left hand:

1. With the thumb in a good position, hammer down your first finger just behind the first fret of the sixth (lowest sounding) string. See how loud a note you can sound with just the left hand.

2. Leaving the first finger where it is, hammer down the second finger behind the second fret. Be sure to be close to it, or the next frets will be difficult to reach.

3. Still leaving each finger on after it has hammered, play successively the third and fourth fingers.

4. Next do the same thing on the fifth string.

5. Following this, play all the remaining strings, hammering as loudly as possible.

Guitar Gods

James Marshall Hendrix was born in Seattle, Washington, on November 27, 1942. Because he was left-handed, he had to teach himself to play the guitar, which he did on an amateur basis through high school. He then entered the Service, where he continued to hone his "chops," and returned to civilian life in 1961. He toured the country playing backup guitar for various R&B acts, including Little Richard and the Isley Brothers. He briefly performed as both a soloist and a leader of Jimmy James and the Blue Flames in the New York area, until moving to England in 1966. There, Chas Chandler of the Animals took him under his wing, introducing him to bassist Noel Redding and drummer Mitch Mitchell; they formed The Jimi Hendrix Experience. Hendrix wowed London with his pyrotechnics, including his use of feedback and distortion and his many unusual playing techniques. He appeared at the Monterey Pop Festival in 1967 and Woodstock in 1969, where he gave memorable performances, set his guitar on fire (at Monterey), and played his famous feedback-drenched version of "The Star-Spangled Banner" (at Woodstock). Hendrix formed the Band of Gypsies with jazz drummer Buddy Miles in 1969, but sadly he died of a drug overdose in September of 1970. Hendrix is perhaps the most influential of all modern rock guitarists, and dozens of posthumous albums have appeared to further his reputation as an experimenter and trendsetter.

This is a wonderful first exercise, because it builds both strength and stretch. Don't be dismayed if you don't produce much sound at first—you'll be amazed at the difference after a few days.

The next step is to put both hands together to play a chord.

The left-hand position

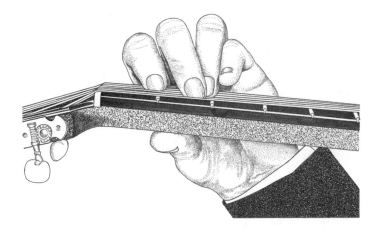

Chords

Chords are groups of notes that, when played together, make a pleasant sound. Chords are used to accompany melodies. Each chord is named for its bass note, and is made up of the first (bass note), third, and fifth notes in a scale. The first thing most people want to learn to do on the guitar is to play simple chords.

The first chord we learn is known as the C chord, since it is built on the bass note C.

Fingering the C chord

Try placing the fingers as in the illustration, keeping the following points in mind:

➤ Press just behind the fret. If you are too far back the string will buzz against the fret.

➤ Keep a slight curve on the fingers—don't let the joints straighten out or give way.

➤ Keep the thumb *behind the neck*, slightly forward of the first fret. Don't bend this joint—keep it back.

➤ Don't press too hard. Accuracy is more important than force.

➤ When you are ready, sound the chord by sweeping your thumb across the upper five strings.

There is a great pleasure in hearing your first chord when the guitar is in tune and resonant. When you have it right, take the hand away and do it again from scratch. Continue until you can find the chord quite easily.

There is a fair amount of detail involved in the correct placement of the left hand, and good habits formed at this stage will pay off tremendously as you continue.

The chord can be shown graphically in various ways. Perhaps the easiest to recognize is the chord block showing part of the guitar fingerboard with round dots representing the fingertips.

A chord block showing the C chord

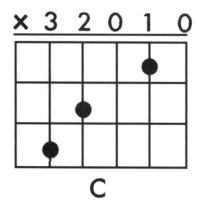

Notice that the fingering is shown by the numbers at the top of the strings. Number 1 represents the index finger, 2 the middle finger, 3 the ring finger, and 4 the little finger. Strings not to be played are marked with an X. The O note denotes an open (unfingered) string. A wide variety of popular music is published with the appropriate chord blocks printed right above the melodies, making this a great and easy way to learn chords. The finger numbers shown here are for the initial learning of chords—sheet music that includes chord blocks will normally show only the dot positions, and the X and 0 markings. This is partially because chords may have different fingerings according to the situation.

Changing Chords

Changing chords takes a lot of practice at first, because the new chord must be found from scratch as quickly as possible. To make this easier, it is important for the fingers to take the shortest route possible from the one chord to the other, while maintaining the general position of the left hand. First, try the G7 chord a few times by itself so as to become familiar with it.

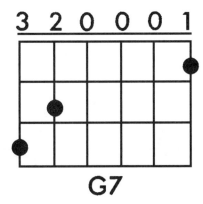

The G7 chord

Notice that the G7 chord uses all six strings.

The next stage is to play a C chord, change to the G7, then back to the C. Here are the points to watch:

➤ Notice that the first finger only has to move a short distance, from the second string to the first. In the same way the second and third fingers also only have to move a distance of one string, from the fourth and fifth to the fifth and sixth.

➤ Try the movement several times with just the left hand. Then, when you feel reasonably familiar with the movement, play the chords with the right-hand thumb as before, remembering that the C chord uses only five strings.

➤ Notice how the G7 chord seems to need to resolve to the C chord. We'll discuss this further at a later point—for now just try to hear the relationship.

After those changes are coming smoothly, try adding the F chord to complete the group most closely related to the C chord. Practice them in the order C, F, G7, C.

Notice that the first finger covers two strings. The technique of covering more than one string with the first finger is known as "barring," as explained below. For now, simply turn the finger sideways so that the pad can cover the two strings.

The F chord

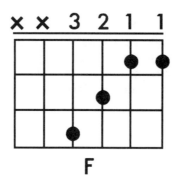

Why These Chords?

The reason that we've chosen to learn the C, F, and G7 chords is that these three chords are commonly used to accompany many, many songs. In fact, there's an entire series of songbooks published using just these three!

Minor Chords

Before moving on to work on the right hand, try these additional chords for further practice. Notice that the letter *m* beside a chord name denotes a minor chord. The plain letter (C, G, etc.) denotes a major chord. Major chords tend to sound brighter and more cheerful, while minor chords have a more melancholy association. Practice in the order Am, Dm, E7, Am.

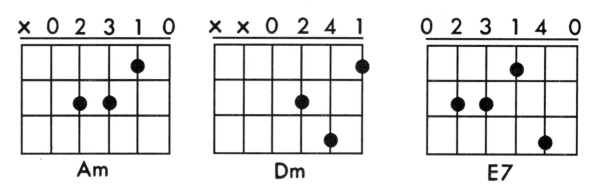

Am, Dm, and E7 chords

As you play these chords, try again to see the "family" relationship between them. Notice that the E7 leads naturally to the A minor. Try to become really familiar with these chords, because we will soon be coordinating them with the right hand to play some songs.

The Least You Need to Know

➤ Proper sitting position—sometimes called classical position—will help you play more easily.

➤ As strength and precision develop in the left hand, chord changes become easier.

➤ Many songs use only three chords, like those illustrated above.

➤ Major chords sound brighter and more cheerful than minor chords.

Chapter 6

The Right Hand

In this Chapter

➤ Establishing a good playing position for the right hand

➤ Preparing the nails

➤ Playing chords

➤ Creating rhythms

➤ Quick review

So far, you've been working on getting your left hand up and running. In this chapter, we'll begin developing your right hand. Establishing good techniques from the very start is crucial, because bad habits, once learned, are difficult to break. You should move slowly through this chapter and make sure you are performing each exercise correctly before continuing. This care will pay off tenfold when you come to the harder exercises later in the book.

Right-Hand Playing Position

It is important to establish a good playing position for the right hand at an early stage. Notice the position of the knuckles, running along the same line as the strings and not at right angles to them. Then see if you can position your hand so that—as you look down— you see the triangle formed between the thumb and first finger. The weight of the arm is taken on top of the guitar; don't let the elbow slide over to the face because this turns the hand into a bad position.

This section is very important for your future progress, and as you are the teacher as well as the student, you should check your position frequently in the early stages.

The right hand as seen from the front

The right hand as the player sees it

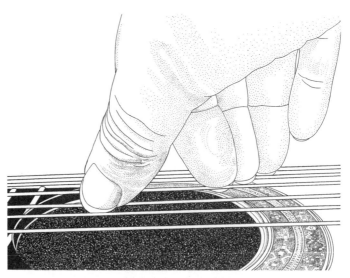

Key Thought
For left-handers, it is possible to reverse the strings and turn the guitar the other way—if you do this, read "right" where you see the word "left." However, I once taught a brilliant left-handed student who preferred to play the conventional, right-handed way.

Preparing the Nails

With a nylon-strung classical guitar, the best sound is produced by playing with the nails. The right-hand nails should be long enough to catch and play the string, but no longer, because a long nail is an impedance and is more likely to break. As a guide, when you look at your hand with the palm facing you, you should see a ridge of nail projecting just above the fingertip and following its contour.

The nails should be shaped with a "diamond dust" or similar nail file, and after shaping a very fine finishing paper (600 grade or better) may be used to polish off any rough edges. The result will be a pure tone with no scratch to it.

Guitar Gods

Charlie Christian was born in Bonham, Texas, on July 29, 1916. His entire family was musical—his parents and brothers were well known in the region for their talents, and young Charlie was soon accompanying them on the guitar. Christian was a legendary jazz guitarist of the thirties and forties, famous for his recordings with Benny Goodman's small groups. He was among the first to play single-note lead lines on an amplified jazz guitar. Christian's crystal-clear lead work and imaginative solo style set the model for jazz guitarists who followed. Famed jazz producer John Hammond featured Christian in the 1939 Carnegie Hall concert known as "From Spirituals to Swing," and this put him on the map as the premiere jazz player. In the early forties, Christian began experimenting with the new bebop style, accompanying Thelonious Monk and Charlie Parker during after-hour sessions at the famous Minton's Playhouse in Harlem, a breeding ground for avant-garde jazz. Sadly, Christian was struck with a paralyzing illness at this same time, and he died of the disease in 1942 in New York City.

Right-Hand Chord Technique

When using a pick or simple thumb strums, the focus is mainly on playing all the available notes of a chord. However, as you progress you will find that you want to select certain notes, and not necessarily those on adjacent strings. This can best be achieved by using the thumb and fingers of the right hand.

To play a chord with the fingers and thumb, first prepare the right hand by selecting the strings to be played. Then squeeze the thumb forward and the fingers back to sound the chord. As the fingers play they will naturally curl upwards, and the thumb will travel slightly upwards and toward the first finger. However, it is not necessary to pull the hand away from the strings, particularly when a succession of chords is to be played, because the hand must quickly be back in position to select the notes for the new chord.

The illustrations show the preparation and completion positions of the chord.

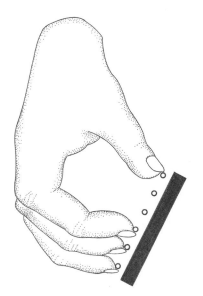

The fingers prepare to play a chord (left). The fingers after the chord has been played (right).

As a practice, try each of the chords you know, choosing the top three strings with the fingers and the lowest note of the chord with the thumb. Remember to ignore the strings where there is an X. Try for a clear, ringing sound.

Rhythmic Variety

Varieties of rhythm, be they blues, waltz, or juapango, are introduced by the varied movements of the right hand. A good pattern to start with is the familiar "oom-pah-pah" of waltz rhythm.

Returning to the C chord, we will play first a single note, the fifth string, with the thumb. Then the index, middle, and ring fingers will play the top three strings together.

Here are the main points:

Pick Hit
The waltz was a dance introduced in Vienna around the turn of the nineteenth century. Originally, dancers were shocked by the notion of such close physical contact between male and female performers; today, the waltz is considered stately and almost prim!

➤ First, find the notes with the left hand, and with the right hand rest the thumb and three fingers on the strings to be played.

➤ With the thumb, don't let the joint bend. Push forward and upward so as to clear the fourth string. Then bring the three fingers out to clear the strings, sounding the notes with the nails as you move through.

➤ Once you can do the movement, play the thumb once and the fingers twice to a count of three. Emphasize the first beat (the thumb stroke) slightly more than the fingers, counting ONE-two-three, ONE-two-three, ONE-two-three, etc.

Further Practice

Once you can do the waltz pattern, try changing the chords from C to G7 and back again. You will find that this is actually easier than playing full chords, because initially you only have one string to find. However, it is good to prepare the complete chord with both hands.

Take Note
Bars are also known as *measures*. A measure is defined by the number of beats that are contained within it. This information is provided at the beginning of the music in the form of a *time signature*.

Next you can try an actual piece—the popular folk song "Clementine." As practiced, the first beat is with the thumb followed by the two chords with the fingers. Notice that the music is divided off by vertical lines known as *bar lines*. The space between the lines represents the *bars* into which music is divided. The divisions make it easier to keep track of the rhythm and stress, because there is a slight accent on the first beat of each measure.

If you know the song "Clementine," try humming or singing along. If not, just play the succession of chords as shown. Where you see the chord name play the thumb, then the two chords.

$\frac{3}{4}$ |C   2   3 |C   2   3 |C   2   3 |G7   2   3

In a | cav - ern   in a | can - yon exca- | va - ting for a | mine _____   dwelt a

|G7   2   3 |C   2   3 |G7   2   3 |C

| mi - ner forty - | ni - ner and his| daugh - ter Clemen- |tine

The Complete Idiot's Reference Card

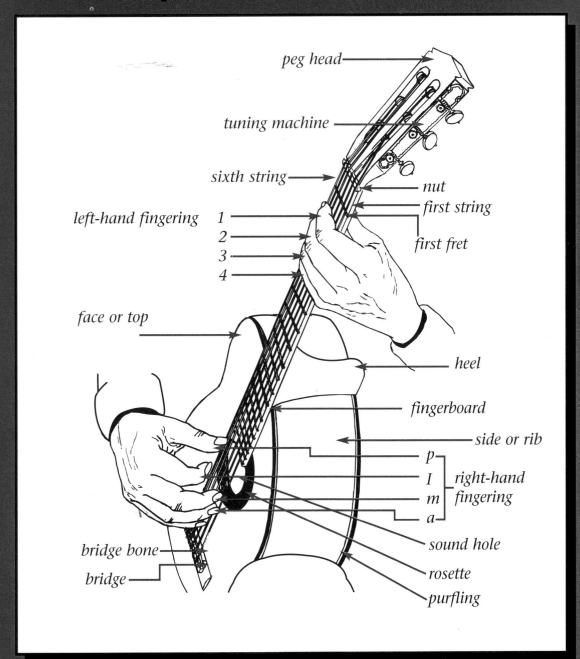

peg head

tuning machine

sixth string

nut

first string

first fret

left-hand fingering

1
2
3
4

face or top

heel

fingerboard

side or rib

p
I
m
a

right-hand fingering

sound hole

rosette

purfling

bridge bone

bridge

ALPHA

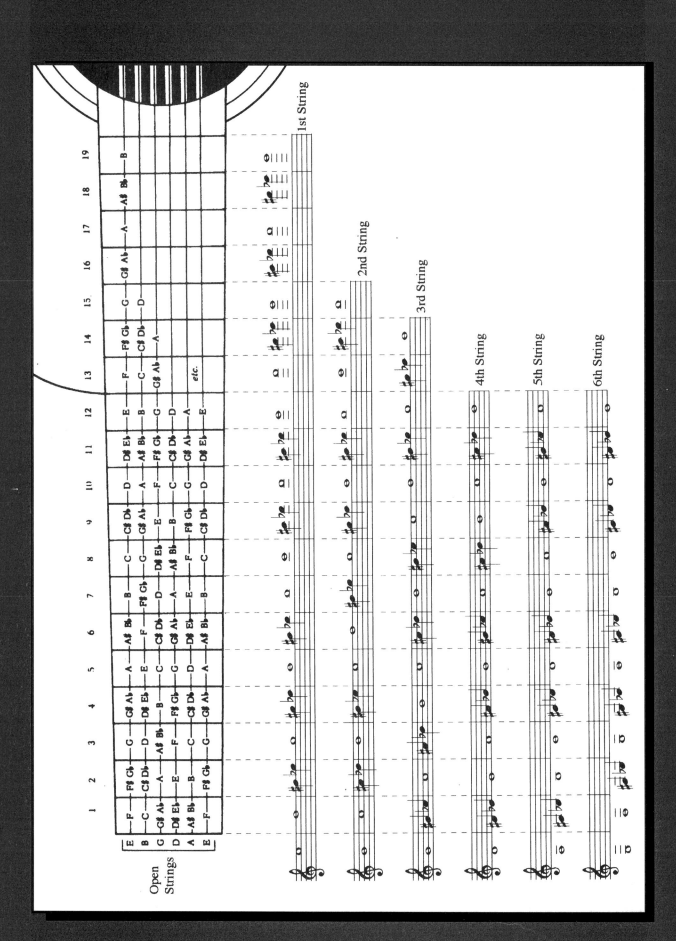

Now see if you can fit the chords to the chorus without all the beats marked.

       C   C   C   G7

Oh my | darling, oh my | darling, oh my | darling Clemen - | tine, Thou art

G7   C   G7   C

lost and gone for | ever, dreadful | sor-ry Clemen - | tine

Quick Review

This is a good time to review what you have learned so far, since the early instruction is fairly intense and there is much to remember. Answering these questions will help the memory.

1. Why use the classical position at this stage?
2. What are the important points related to positioning the guitar?
3. Can you play the C, F, G7, Am, and Dm chords?
4. Are chords played with the fingertips or the nails?
5. To see your hands, should you lean your head forward or pull the guitar back?
6. What is a bar line? Why is it used?

The Least You Need to Know

➤ Holding the right hand over the strings in the proper position will help you play more easily.
➤ Classical guitar players need to keep their nails carefully shaped, just long enough to play the strings.
➤ How to play simple chords.
➤ How to add rhythm to your chord progressions.
➤ How to play in waltz rhythm.

Chapter 7

Advanced Right-Hand Techniques

In this Chapter

➤ Learning the rest stroke

➤ Alternating fingers

➤ Melodies and arpeggios

➤ Learning the free stroke

➤ Playing arpeggios

Now that you have some playing experience under your belt, we can move ahead to some more interesting playing styles. This chapter covers the basics of playing individual notes, rather than just strumming chords. To learn to play melodies, we have to learn more sophisticated right-hand playing techniques.

This chapter introduces two of the more common styles of playing individual notes: the rest stroke and the free stroke. By learning these techniques, you will be able to play notes cleanly and easily, with a full sound. These techniques will lay the basis for all of your future playing, so we will break down their components so you can quickly understand and master them.

The Rest Stroke

Up to now, most of what we have covered could be played with a pick, but we will be studying arpeggios that are much easier to play with the fingers. For the single-note melodies that follow, a pick could be used, but now is a good moment to learn the principal stroke used for melody lines on the finger-style and classical guitar, known as the *rest stroke*.

The rest stroke is the technique that produces the fullest sound from a single note. It is played by plucking the string in such a way that, when the movement is completed, the fingertip comes to rest on the adjacent string—hence the name.

Here are the steps:

➤ The fingertip is placed on the string in preparation.

➤ As the nail passes the string it catches and sounds the note.

➤ The fingertip ends the movement on the next string.

➤ It is most important to keep the finger slightly curved—do *not* let the joint yield as the nail plays the note, because this will weaken your attack.

The rest stroke

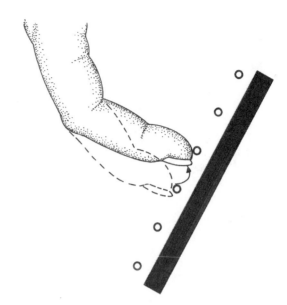

The rest stroke is quite a subtle movement, because small adjustments can mean a considerable improvement in tone quality. It is fun to experiment with this, and good habits developed at this stage will ensure maximum progress. Take a look at it now from another angle. This picture shows the nail sliding off the string at a slight angle, with the finger slanted so as to engage the string with less-than-maximum nail. This change in axis from a head-on approach softens the attack of the finger to produce a more delicate sound.

The finger is angled to engage less of the nail.

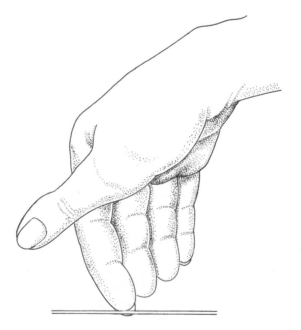

Try these movements out now to see if you can produce a full and beautiful sound. Remember that the state of the nail is important since rough areas will catch and produce a grating sound.

Here are the main points to remember:

➤ Prepare to play by positioning the finger on the fingertip with the nail projecting over the string.

➤ Press the string down slightly before playing.

➤ For a strong attack, play with more nail, i.e., with the center of the nail.

➤ For a subtler sound angle the nail and the stroke.

Alternation

As a general rule, the same finger does not perform successive rest strokes. It takes too much time to prepare the same finger for a second stroke when another finger could be ready to start. The commonest way to play a passage of single notes is to alternate the index *(i)* and middle *(m)* fingers. The motion is like walking the fingers in place—as one plays, the other moves back to be ready for the next note.

Practical Work

As a first experiment, try playing a succession of notes on the top string, starting with *i* and alternating with *m*. Try to keep the notes even and matching each other in sound. Then do the same thing starting with *m*.

Note that some players, particularly those specializing in flamenco, develop a preference for starting single-note runs with a particular finger, usually *i*. This is in fact counterproductive because the best finger for starting a run depends on the specific passage.

Now try the second string, playing *i-m-i-m-i-m-i-m*, then *m-i-m-i-m-i-m-i*.

Finally, do the same practice on the third string.

After that, try the same exercise that you did with the left hand alone, playing the first four frets of each string, this time with both hands.

When you reach the highest note, come back down the guitar playing the frets in the order four, three, two, one on all the strings. This makes an excellent daily warm-up exercise.

If you try the string changes reversing the fingers, i.e., using *i-m* where I have suggested *m-i*, you will find making the change from string to string harder. This is a basic principle of fingering—where possible, we cross strings as shown above. However, we need to be able to do it both ways, because the easy method of crossing is not always practical.

The Free Stroke

The *free stroke* is used in chords, in arpeggios as demonstrated below, and in single-note situations where the rest stroke is not practical. It differs from the rest stroke in that the finger comes clear of the adjacent string at the end of the movement.

Successive notes played with the free stroke use alternation in the same way. Try playing the exercise that you did with the rest stroke and you will notice the different sound. Good players are able to develop a full sound that almost has the quality of a rest stroke.

The free stroke

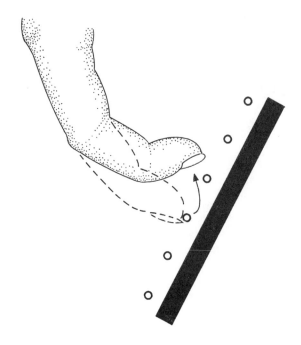

Arpeggios

When the notes of a chord are played in succession rather than together the expression *arpeggio* is used.

At its simplest, an arpeggio can mean simply playing the notes of the chord one after the other. For the upward arpeggio this can be achieved with precision if the notes of the chord are prepared in advance.

Here is how to do a simple upward arpeggio with open strings:

➤ Prepare both hands as if to play a chord

➤ Play the sixth string with the thumb, without moving the fingers. Do a rest stroke, and leave the thumb on the fifth string. This helps to support the hand.

➤ Play the index finger note (the third string), leaving the middle and ring fingers in place. Use a free stroke.

➤ Play the middle-finger note (the second string), leaving the ring finger in place. (This is more tricky.)

➤ Finally, play the first string with the ring finger.

➤ Replace thumb and fingers, ready to start again.

Here is a pictorial representation of the movements.

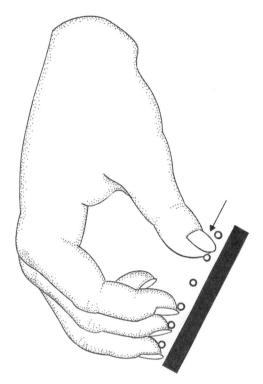

After all fingers are prepared the thumb plays.

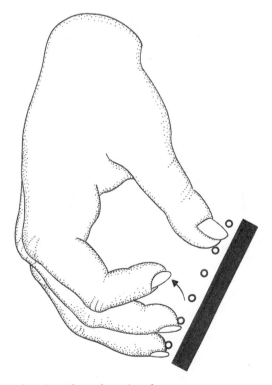

Next, the index finger plays, leaving the others in place.

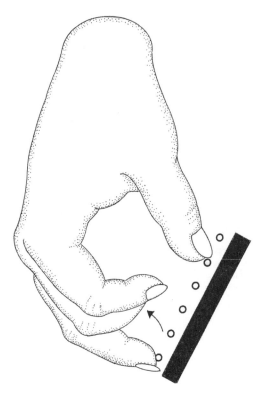

The middle finger plays, without any movement of the ring finger.

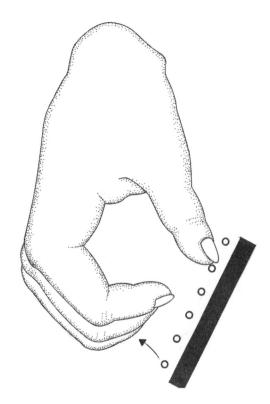

The ring finger plays.

The right-hand fingers are usually indicated by the first letters of their Italian or Spanish names. They are easy to remember since *i* and *m* are used for the index and middle fingers. For the ring or *annular* finger *a* is used, and the thumb is represented by *p* (for the Spanish *pulgar*). Thus the right-hand fingering for the above arpeggio would be *p-i-m-a*.

p	thumb
i	index
m	middle
a	annular (ring) finger

Practice the *p-i-m-a* arpeggio until you can do it smoothly, and then try it on the other chords, remembering to use the thumb on the appropriate strings. Choose the lowest one for the thumb and the top three for the fingers.

For the reverse arpeggio *p-a-m-i*, it is not necessary to place all the fingers in advance. Just the outside fingers, *p* and *a*, are sufficient.

After becoming reasonably familiar with the physical movements involved for chords, arpeggios, and single-note alternation, it is time to play some actual tunes and accompaniments, and to do this we need to learn ways that the tunes can be written down. Then we can move on to learning songs and chording.

The Least You Need to Know

➤ How to perform a rest stroke.

➤ How to perform a free stroke.

➤ How to alternate the fingers to play a series of notes.

➤ How an arpeggio is made out of a chord.

➤ The standard way of referring to the fingers of the right hand: *p* for thumb, *i* for index, *m* for middle, and *a* for ring.

Part 3
Tunes and Tablature

So far, so good. We've learned and practiced some basic techniques for both hands. Now it's time to learn how to read guitar tablature—the simplest method for notating (writing down) guitar music. This notation enables us to recognize notes quickly and easily. Then we can practice the new techniques by playing some familiar songs. After working on different time values, we add valuable new skills to our repertoire in Chapter 10—the left-hand hammer-on and pull-off.

Chapter 8

How Guitar Music Is Written

In this Chapter

➤ What is tablature?

➤ How do you read it?

➤ Understanding time signatures

➤ Counting the beat

➤ Learning basic note values

➤ Understanding fractional beats

➤ Playing some simple songs

Written music can serve many purposes. It can help us remember what we have heard once before. But it can also help us learn something we've never heard—and thus expand our musical horizons.

Luckily, guitar tablature—the easiest way of writing down music for the guitar—is simple to understand, once you know the basics. It can be your doorway to an entirely new world of music. So let's spend a few minutes familiarizing ourselves with the basics of tablature.

Guitar Tablature

In the earliest days, music for the guitar was written in a form known as *tablature*. This system indicates exactly where the fingers are to be placed by showing the strings as six lines, with numbers (or letters) representing the frets. Here is an example:

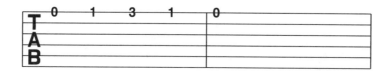

➤ The word TAB is conventionally placed at the beginning of the line to distinguish these lines from those of the musical staff. Here, the lines represent the six strings, the first string being the top line.

➤ "0" stands for open string. Play the first string with the right hand; do nothing with the left.

➤ "1" stands for the first fret. Place a finger behind the first fret on the same string. Play the note.

➤ "3" stands for the third fret. Finger the third fret, play the note.

➤ The vertical line marks off the measures, as in conventional notation.

Note that the numbers have nothing to do with the fingers. In this example they happen to coincide, but they refer only to the frets.

Now try playing these examples in succession:

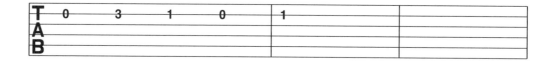

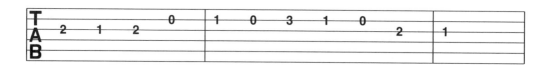

If something sounds familiar, you're doing well!

The rhythm can be expressed in various ways in tablature, but before discussing this we need to learn some basics in this area.

Rhythm and Counting

The length of individual notes is easy to express simply by having a different symbol for each length. Also, it is necessary to specify periods of silence when required between notes. These silences are called *rests,* and they have symbols corresponding to the duration of the notes. Here are the common ones.

Whole		
Half		
Quarter		
Eighth		
Sixteenth		
Thirtysecond		
Sixtyfourth		

Notes and their equivalent rests

A dot placed after any note increases its length by half.

As previously mentioned, music is conventionally divided off into *measures* or *bars*. We usually prefer to use the term *measure*, because, as we shall see later, *bar* has an alternative meaning in guitar music.

Time Signatures

Measures can be of different lengths to accommodate different rhythms. The initial measure length is specified at the beginning of the piece. It takes the form of a fraction, the upper number expressing how many beats in each measure, and the lower one the length of each beat. Here's how it looks:

$$\frac{4}{4}$$

This indicates four beats to the measure (the upper number). The lower number specifies that each beat has a duration of a quarter note. We call this "four four time." This is the most common time in music, so is often shown by the abbreviation

C

$\frac{3}{8}$

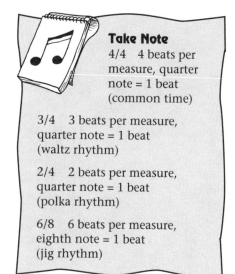

Take Note

4/4 4 beats per measure, quarter note = 1 beat (common time)

3/4 3 beats per measure, quarter note = 1 beat (waltz rhythm)

2/4 2 beats per measure, quarter note = 1 beat (polka rhythm)

6/8 6 beats per measure, eighth note = 1 beat (jig rhythm)

The three on top indicates that there will be three beats. The eight below shows that each beat will last an eighth note. We would refer to this as "three eight time."

How to Count Time

Knowledge of the mathematical lengths of the notes is only useful up to a point. More important is how to relate these to the onward flow of the music, and this is done by counting the beats. It is the same as beating time to music that you hear—you respond to the beats and tap your foot accordingly. But when you become the player, you have to establish your own beat to set the time.

Here are some examples to put this into practice:

First count these measures evenly as shown, with a slight extra stress on the first beat of each one.

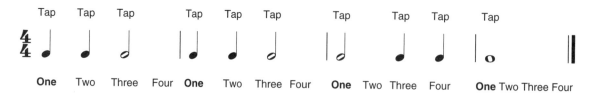

Now try these measures with varying note lengths. See if you can tap out the notes while keeping an even count., i.e.:

Here is an example in 3/4 time. Notice the dot after the half note which increases its time by half again. Thus, it gets three counts instead of two:

58

Now let's try this with the guitar, playing the tablature notes instead of just tapping. Use alternating rest strokes for the melody (counting practice #1):

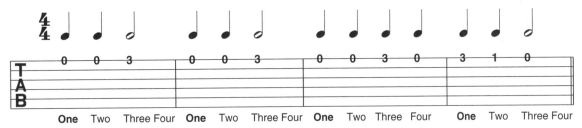

It is very important to try to count at the same time as you play. It seems a lot to remember at this stage, but if you try it a few times you will find it becomes quite natural. This will help tremendously later, when you start reading regular music notation.

Now here is an example in 3/4 time (counting practice #2):

Be careful in the second to last measure, where the rhythm is a little different.

Ties, Rests, and Damping

Tunes do not always fit neatly into measures, and sometimes we want to hold over a note from one measure to the next. This is easily done by writing the extra amount as a note in the next measure and *tying* the two notes together, like this:

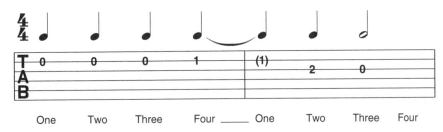

In the example, the first fret note is held over through the first beat of the next measure. In practice the tied note will often not be shown in the tablature, so it is important to spot it in the note indications.

Rests are simply silences, but they must have a time value, like notes, and fit into the measures in the same way:

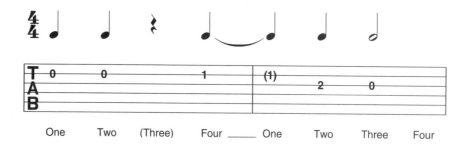

One two (three) four __ one two three four

In the example, the third beat is silent, so the string should be damped. If it was not an open string, it would be sufficient just to lift the left-hand finger. However, to stop the open string from ringing on, it is necessary to touch it lightly. This can be done here with a left-hand finger or with the side of the right-hand thumb.

Some Familiar Tunes

Now is the time to try some well-known tunes. See if you can play them in time and recognize some of them. Remember to count as well as play.

"Au Clair de la Lune"

"Drink to Me Only with Thine Eyes"

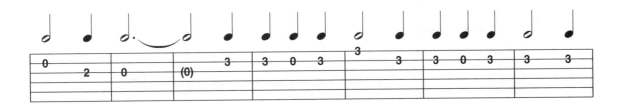

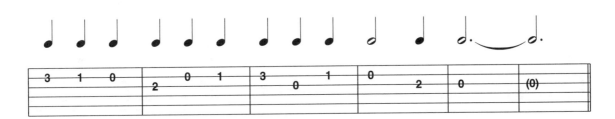

Most tunes need faster notes, so now is a good moment to see how these are written and counted.

The Eighth Note

Up to now, it has been possible to count the measures by giving each of the notes one or more counts. The same applies to eighth notes when the time signature has an eight as the lower number. For instance, 6/8 measures are counted like this:

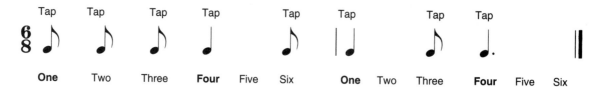

The differences to notice here are:

➤ There are two stresses in 6/8, on the first and fourth beats. The stress on the first beat is slightly heavier than the stress on the fourth.

➤ Because the eighth note is the counting unit, the quarter note, which lasts as long as two eighth notes, now gets two counts.

➤ The dotted quarter note counts half as much again, i.e., it gets three counts.

When faster notes are grouped together, they are frequently joined together to make them easier to read. For instance, the above would normally be written like this:

Try counting and tapping out the rhythm for the above example. When you can do this you will be able to play this tune in 6/8.

Nursery Rhyme

If you recognize this well-known nursery rhyme, you are doing well.

Counting Beats with Fractions

So far, all the notes we have counted have lasted one or more beats. Often, however, more than one note occupies a beat, and we have to have a way to count this. For instance, in 4/4 time the beats are counted in quarter notes, so the eighth note will only last a half beat. Here is the way that this is usually counted:

One   Two and Three   Four

The pulse of the one-two-three-four remains even, but the "and" introduces another syllable between the main beats. Groups of faster notes are usually joined together with a thicker line known as a *beam,* which makes them easier to recognize. The number of beams corresponds to the number of flags on individual notes. Eighth notes have a single flag, so they are connected as shown below. Try counting and playing these combinations:

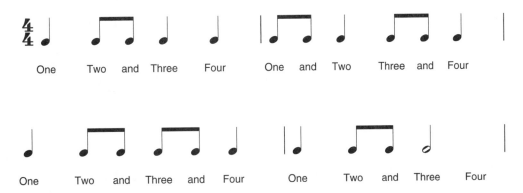

Now here is a song for counting practice. Notice that it does not begin on the first note of a measure, but in fact on an unstressed "pickup" note that is the last beat of an incomplete measure. Count "Three" on this, then "One" as usual on the first beat of the following measure.

When a piece begins with an incomplete measure, the balance of the time is made up in the last measure, which here has only two counts. First and last incomplete measures always add up to one complete one.

"The Ash Grove"

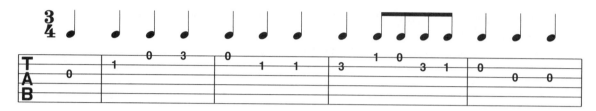

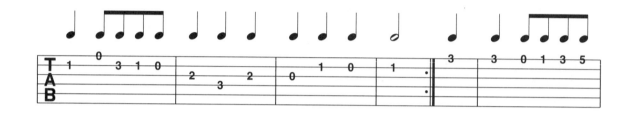

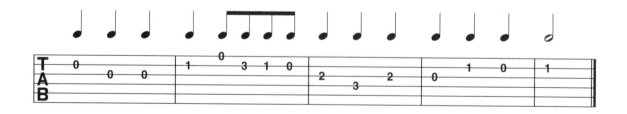

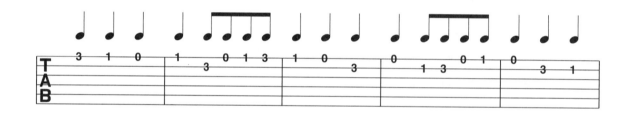

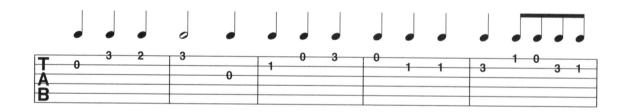

More about Dotted Notes

We have seen that putting a dot after a note increases its length by half, and thus that the dotted quarter note lasts for a quarter note and a half, or a quarter plus an eighth. When the eighth note was the beat, as in "The Ash Grove," there was no problem because the dotted quarter lasted for three eighth-note beats. But what if the count is in quarter notes, as in 4/4 time? The dotted quarter will now have one and a half beats, and we have to find a way to count this.

Here is how it is done:

One   Two   and   Three

The quarter note lasts into the next beat, so we count the next number while holding the note. If the dotted quarter is followed by an eighth note (as it frequently is), the eighth note would be on the second half of the second beat, so it would be counted with an "and."

Try counting and tapping these examples.

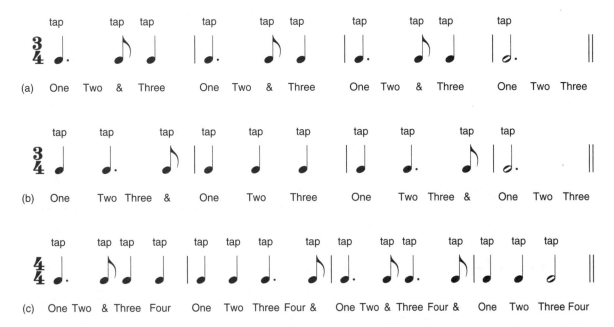

It is worth persisting with the above two examples until you really understand the count. The dotted quarter note is the hardest one for most beginners to count.

Now try counting and playing these examples.

"Greensleeves"

"Muss I Denn"

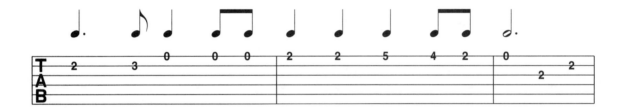

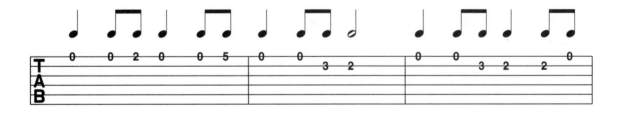

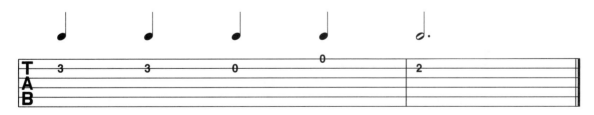

The sign ⦂‖ means repeat—in this case, go back to the beginning.

Irish Air: "Endearing Young Charms"

The Least You Need to Know

➤ Tablature is a system of showing how to play pieces on the guitar.

➤ The six lines of guitar tablature correspond to the six strings.

➤ Time signatures are used to indicate the number of beats per measure, and which note receives a single beat.

➤ Common time is 4/4.

➤ It is important to be able to count the beats properly, and to hold each note for its correct length, in order to play a melody.

➤ When playing a dotted note, the total time value is increased by half—so in common time a dotted quarter note is held for one and a half beats.

Chapter 9

Varied Accompaniments

In this Chapter

➤ Basic accompaniments in tablature

➤ Some familiar songs:

➤ "Down in the Valley"

➤ "The Riddle Song"

➤ "The Streets of Laredo"

➤ "Aura Lee"

➤ "Waltzing Matilda"

➤ A first classical solo

Well, we've come a long way since we were first learning to play chords. By using more complicated right-hand patterns, learning to move from chord to chord, and learning to read tablature, we've already been able to play some familiar songs and enjoy them.

Now we're ready to combine these talents so we can play some broken chords using tablature. This will enable us to play even more songs, and to begin to understand how to make our own chord arrangements—so we can play in any style that we'd like.

As an added bonus, the chapter ends with our very first guitar solo. This classical piece will put all your fingers to the test—but don't worry, you'll be ready for it!

Playing Chords and Arpeggios in Tablature

Now that we understand the basics of counting, it becomes possible to try out some variations of chords and arpeggios. Here, for instance, is the waltz time discussed in Chapter 8:

Waltz Tempo

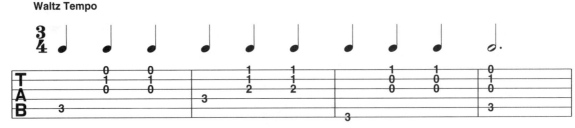

And here's an easy and useful arpeggio in eighth notes:

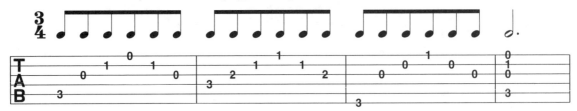

Chords and arpeggios are often mixed, like this:

The best way to see the possibilities is to work on some familiar songs. First, simply play the chords from the chord symbols while humming or singing the tune. Then play from the tablature. You will actually find the tablature a little easier, because you will see that it is often unnecessary to play all the notes of a chord, and the actual accompaniments are simpler in texture.

Guitar Gods

Huddie Ledbetter, better known as Leadbelly, was born in the small town of Mooringsport, Louisiana, on January 29, 1889. From a young age, he was a strong laborer and talented player of the guitar, but he was also quick to anger and got into many fights. He traveled through Louisiana and neighboring states, performing at roadhouses and parties. However, his hard living and bad temper got the better of him, and he ended up in prison twice, working on the chain gang for charges of murder and attempted murder. While he was a prison inmate in Mississippi, Leadbelly was "discovered" by folklorists John and Alan Lomax. They realized he was an excellent player of the 12-string guitar. Leadbelly then went to New York and became a popular performer, playing a mix of blues and songs from his childhood. One of his favorites was "Down in the Valley," which he did much to popularize. He also arranged the old popular song "Good Night, Irene" in a version that, ironically, became a major top-of-the-pops hit for the folk group the Weavers, just a year after Leadbelly's death in 1949.

"Down in the Valley" (Folk Song from Kentucky)

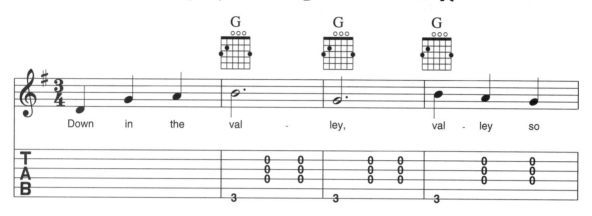

Down   in   the   val   -   ley,   val   -   ley   so

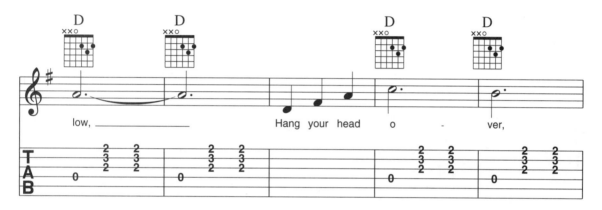

low, _____   Hang your head   o   -   ver,

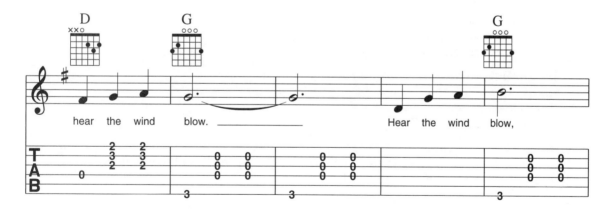

hear the wind   blow. _____   Hear the wind   blow,

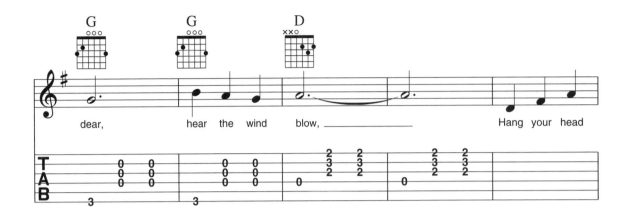

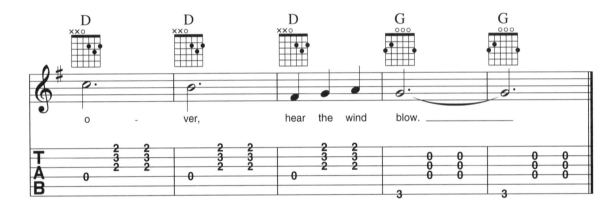

Additional lyrics:

Write me a letter, containing three lines,
Answer my question, will you be mine?
Will you be mine, dear, will you be mine?
Answer my question, will you be mine?

Roses love sunshine, violets love dew,
Angels in heaven, know I love you.
Know I love you, dear, know I love you,
Angels in heaven, know I love you.

This piece is in straightforward waltz time, as practiced above. When you try the tablature, you will notice that I am using an easy version of the G chord that leaves out the top note, but it sounds very resonant with the three open strings.

For the final verse, leave out the last two beats of the last measure, playing either a full chord or just the bass note on the first beat.

"The Riddle Song"

Additional lyrics:

How can there be a cherry that has no stone?
How can there be a chicken that has no bone?
How can there be a story that has no end?
How can there be a baby with no cryin'?

A cherry when it's blooming it has no stone.
A chicken when it's pipen, it has no bone,
The story of I love you, it has no end,
And a baby when it's sleeping, there's no cryin'.

After playing it through with the chords, try the tablature version. This very simple arpeggio works well, and it demonstrates how sometimes less can be more.

"The Streets of Laredo" (Traditional Cowboy Song)

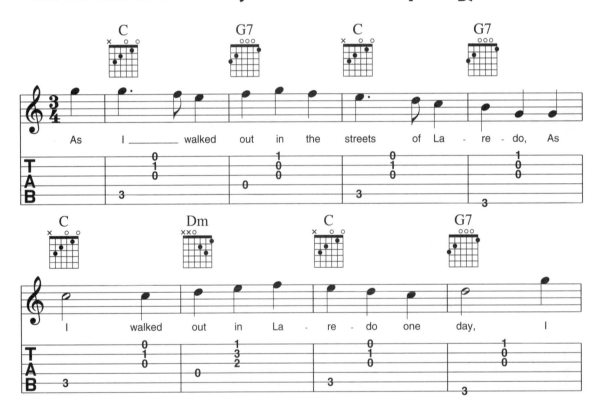

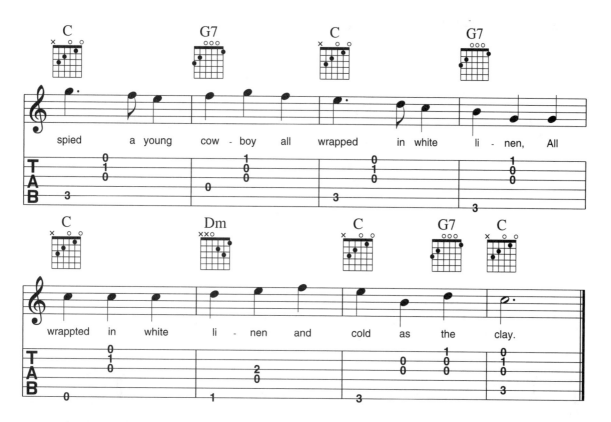

spied   a young   cow - boy   all   wrapped   in white   li - nen,   All

wrappted   in   white   li - nen   and   cold   as   the   clay.

Additional lyrics:

It was once in the saddle I used to go dashing,
It was once in the saddle I used to go gay.
First to the dram-house and then to the card-house,
Got shot in the breast and I'm dying today.

Get six jolly cowboys to carry my coffin,
Get six pretty maidens to bear up my pall.
Put bunches of roses all over my coffin,
Put roses to deaden the sods as they fall.

We beat the drum slowly and played the fife lowly,
And bitterly we wept as we bore him along.
For we all loved our comrade, so brave, young and handsome,
We all loved our comrade although he'd done wrong.

When playing from the tablature, let the second chord in each measure ring through. The correct timing would be:

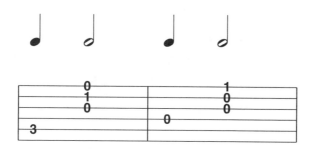

"Aura Lee" (George Poulton, Lyrics by W. W. Fosdick)

Additional lyrics:

On her cheek the rose was born,
'Twas music when she spoke,
In her eyes the rays of morn,
With sudden splendor broke.

Aura Lee! Aura Lee!
Maid of golden hair,
Sunshine came along with thee,
And swallows in the air.

Some New Chords

This song introduces two new chords, B7 and A7, commonly fingered as below.

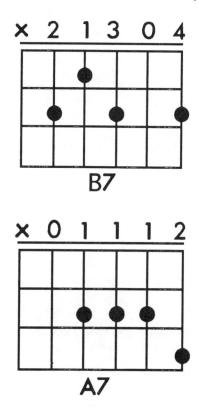

The A7 chord involves a larger half bar than that used for the F chord—care should be taken over the position.

The Half Bar

The half bar

After you study the illustrations, bear these points in mind:

➤ The finger should be right up to the fret.

➤ Arrange the finger so that the crease at the first joint lies between the strings. If the crease lies right on the string it may cause a muffled sound.

➤ Always remember that a lot of pressure is a mistake, and not necessary when a good position is established.

The term *half bar* is slightly misleading, because it is used for the barring of any number of strings from two to five. Logically, when all six strings are barred this is known as a full bar.

The final song accompaniment at this stage is the rollicking "Waltzing Matilda" from Australia.

"Waltzing Matilda" (A. B. "Banjo" Patterson)

Additional lyrics:

Down came a jumbuck to drink at that billabong,
Up jumped the swagman and grabbed him with glee,
And he sang as he shoved that jumbuck in his tuckerbag,
You'll come a waltzing Matilda with me.

Chorus:

Waltzing Matilda, Waltzing Matilda,
You'll come a waltzing Matilda with me,
And he sang as he watched and he waited while his billy boiled,
You'll come a waltzing Matilda with me.

Up rode the squatter mounted on his thoroughbred,
Down came the troopers, one, two, three,
Who's that jolly jumbuck you've got in your tuckerbag?
You'll come a waltzing Matilda with me.

Up jumped the swagman, sprang into the billabong,
You'll never catch me alive said he,
And his ghost may be heard as you pass beside that billabong,
You'll come a waltzing Matilda with me.

A First Solo

After practicing the songs it is time to try a solo. The "Andantino" was written by the famous nineteenth-century teacher and composer Ferdinando Carulli, who was a leading figure of the guitar world in Paris at a time when the guitar was in great vogue.

I have included the standard notation to show both the timing and the fingering, since these tend to clutter up the tablature line. The notes are no more difficult than the accompaniments you've already practiced, and the piece should provide a pleasant recreation.

As before, the two dots by the double bar :‖ indicate a repeat. The first half repeats from the beginning, then the second half repeats back to where the dots and double bar point the other way ‖: .

FINE marks the end of the piece.

"Andantino" (Ferdinando Carulli)

Moderate Tempo

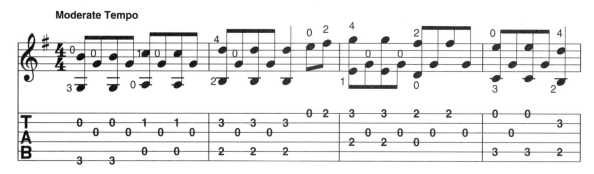

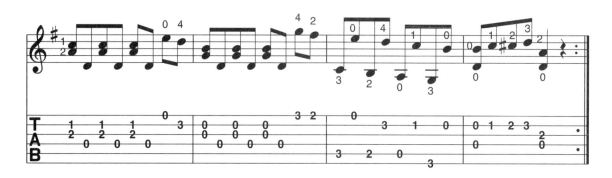

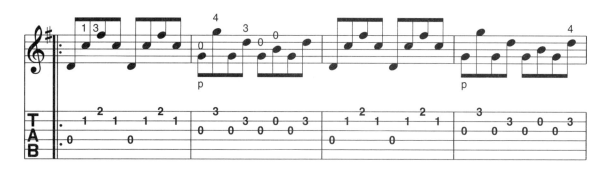

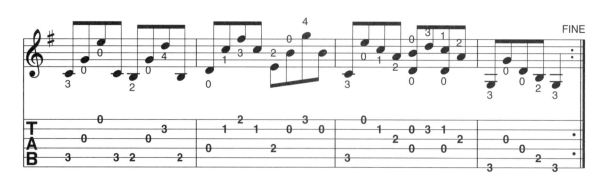

The Least You Need to Know

➤ How to accompany yourself using basic arpeggios and chords.

➤ How to read chord symbols and their representation in tablature.

➤ Understanding how sometimes "less is more" when working out an accompaniment.

➤ Some basic fingering styles for chord accompaniment.

Chapter 10

Rhythm Practice

In this Chapter

➤ Counting faster notes

➤ Introducing sixteenth notes

➤ Mixed rhythms

➤ Triplets

Most guitarists want to play fast—but, truth be told, it's not the speed of the "guitar gods" that impresses us, it's rather the *evenness* with which they play each note. Playing fast is easy; playing in rhythm is hard.

We've already begun to experience some quicker time values in our study of eighth notes. This chapter will take us further, into the speedier world of sixteenth notes and triplets. As always, playing slowly and evenly is far more important than burning up the strings.

As you progress through this chapter, the temptation will be to pick up speed. That's fine, as long as you remember to keep playing evenly!

Advanced Counting

Soon we will be learning to read standard musical notation, and this will be *much* easier if we already have a solid grasp of counting. Beginners usually have more trouble reading the time than the actual notes, but we have already made a good start by learning to count quarter and eighth notes.

Guitar Gods

Chester Burton Atkins was born on June 20, 1924, near the small town of Luttrell, Tennessee. Chet took up fiddle as a youngster, but switched to guitar by the time he was a teenager, when he got his first jobs touring with country singers Archie Campbell and Bill Carlisle. He began recording in the late forties, establishing his unique style of playing: he used his thumb with a pick to play the lower strings, establishing a rhythm, and then played the melodies on the upper strings with his fingers. His early recordings of boogie-influenced pieces were highly influential on a new generation of country players who were influenced by jazz and pop music.

In the 1950s, Atkins became better known as a recording executive in Nashville than as a musician, although he played on many sessions. He continued in this work through the sixties, helping to establish a smooth, jazz-influenced style known as the Nashville Sound. Meanwhile, in the seventies, he was "rediscovered" as a guitarist, and over the next few decades he made influential recordings with everyone from pioneers like Les Paul to newcomers like Mark Knopfler.

Now it is time to count faster notes, and to recognize and play some of the rhythmic patterns that you will be encountering frequently. In addition, we will learn to count and play triplets—groups of three notes that share a beat.

Sixteenth Notes

The next level of counting involves sixteenths, which logically enough are played twice as fast as eighths. Again there is a traditional way of counting which makes it quite simple to sort out mixtures of different time values.

Reviewing what we have learned already, we use the number for the main beats, and for faster notes in between we use the word *and*. Now, to double up again, we use the short syllables *e* and *a* like this:

When you count, start with a slow four, then keep the number counts at the same steady pace as you fill in the sounds for the other notes.

Smaller Note Values Do Not Always Equal Greater Speed

Sixteenths are twice as fast as eighths; however, they may not indicate a fast piece. Bach often used sixteenths in very slow pieces. The final speed is determined by the *tempo* marking at the beginning of the piece. Here are the most common, some of which indicate mood as well as speed:

largo	broad, slow
lento	slow
andante	walking, leisurely
moderato	moderate speed
allegretto	cheerful, fairly fast
allegro	cheerful, faster than allegretto
vivace	lively, a lively speed
presto	fast
prestissimo	very fast

In a piece marked "prestissimo" a quarter note may be played very rapidly, whereas in a piece marked "largo" a sixteenth note would be played very slowly. However, the relationship between quarters, eighths, and sixteenths remains the same; it is just the tempo or basic beat of the piece that is increased or diminished.

Mixed Rhythms

Now here are some mixed examples. Count and tap them out until you see clearly how they relate to the rhythm.

One   and   a   Two   and   a   Three   and   a   Four

"William Tell"

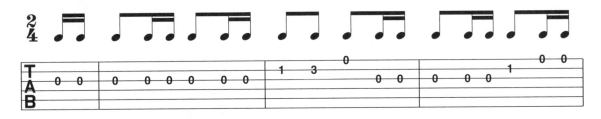

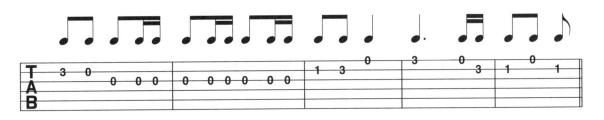

One   e   and   Two   and   Three   e   and   Four

"Leaves So Green"

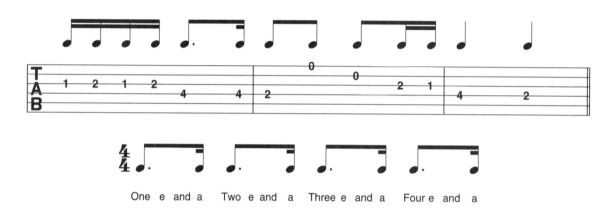

One e and a   Two e and a   Three e and a   Four e and a

When you understand the rhythm try leaving out the "e and," counting simply:

One   a Two   a Three, etc.

"Humoresque"

Triplets

Sometimes we need to divide notes into uneven amounts. The commonest example of this is the *triplet,* in which three notes occupy a single beat. Here is the conventional count in common time:

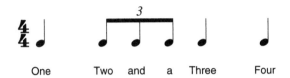

The number counts are evenly spaced as usual. The "Two-and-a" should be an even three occupying the second beat. Try tapping it out as well. Then see if you can work out the study below.

It is very important to understand the triplets, because we will be using them extensively in all styles of music.

The Least You Need to Know

➤ Sixteenths are twice as fast as eighths.

➤ Mixed eighths and sixteenths can be counted easily using special words.

➤ Triplets divide the beat into three parts. There is a simple way to count them.

➤ The actual speed of a piece is indicated by its *tempo* marking.

Slur Techniques

The Upward Slur (Hammer-On, Ascending Ligado)

Slurs are fun. They are easy to do and open up all sorts of new musical possibilities. The slur is a means of linking one note to another in a way that sounds smoother than playing each note separately. Upward slurs are known colloquially as hammer-ons, and downward slurs as pull-offs, for reasons that will become obvious.

First let's learn the upward (hammer-on) slur. What we want to do is to link two notes together where the second is higher in pitch than the first.

For example, let's move from the open top string to the note one fret above:

The curved line between the two notes shows how slurs are written in both tablature and standard notation. To play this example, first play the open first string, then hammer the left-hand first finger down to sound the note at the first fret. Because the first fret is played only with the left hand, it is necessary to bring the finger down smartly with enough force to sound the note. Notice that the two notes sound linked together compared with the two notes played separately by the right hand. Try doing it both ways to hear the effect.

Remember these technique points:

➤ The hammer must be strong enough to sound the second note clearly.

➤ The finger that hammers starts from a point not too far from the string, not more than $1/2$ to $3/4$ inch. Otherwise you could miss the string, or at least the exact point that you want to strike. You will get the best sound hammering just behind the fret.

➤ Hammer with the tip of the finger, not the side.

Now try from one fret to another instead of just slurring from the open string.

Put the left-hand first finger on the F at the first fret. Play the note, then hammer firmly with the third finger. Practice until you hear two distinct sounds.

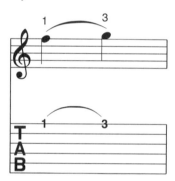

Now try practicing this exercise. When you see the number 5 in the tablature simply slide the third finger up to it, and then back to the 3. We'll be learning more about position-changing soon.

Guitar Gods

Blind Blake was born c. 1895, probably in Jacksonville, Florida. Little is known of the blind ragtime guitarist's life, although it is believed he traveled from Florida to Georgia as a teenager, and was living and working in Chicago by the twenties. He was a prolific recording artist, recording over 80 titles on his own, and also providing many accompaniments for other blues singers.

Blake's style drew on East Coast ragtime riffs. He produced a particularly snappy bass line, with unique improvised melodic fragments placed above it. Although he relied on similar patterns in many of his songs, the overall effect was quite contemporary and jazzy, and his work was much admired. He also recorded with boogie pianist Charlie Spann in the late twenties, where his guitar work perfectly complemented Spann's complex piano lines.

Just as little is known of Blake's life, little is known of his death. Some believe he froze to death on the streets of Chicago in the early thirties, others think he was killed in an accident.

Upward Slur Exercise

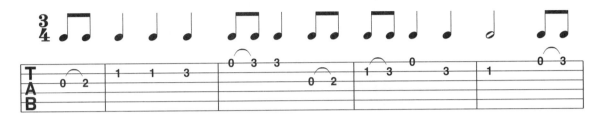

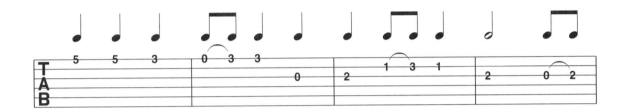

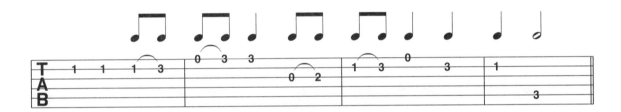

The Downward Slur (Pull-Off, Descending Ligado)

The term *pull-off* gives a clue to the technique of the downward slur. The first note is played, then the left-hand finger pulls away, plucking the string as it goes.

Here is how it looks in tablature and standard notation:

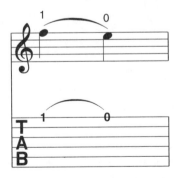

It is important to remember that the left hand actually *plucks* the second note. Many beginners just lift the finger off, resulting in a weak slur. Try it now, and really sound the open string.

Where two fretted notes are involved, both fingers must be in position before starting the slur, otherwise the second note will be indistinct.

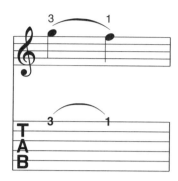

Place the first finger firmly behind the first fret. Then put the third finger on, play the note with the right hand, and *pluck* the finger away to sound the lower note.

Slurs on Inside Strings

When slurring is between notes on the inside strings, in most cases you will pluck *downwards*, with the finger ending up on the fingerboard and in contact with the adjacent string. An exception is the rare case in which the upper string is meant to continue sounding. To avoid damping the upper string, pull sideways so that the finger clears the other string.

To practice these points, try this example.

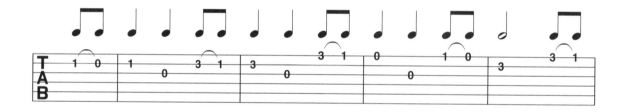

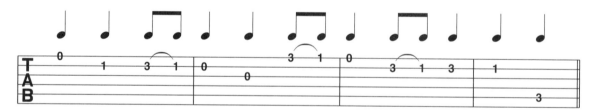

Downward Slur Exercise

One of the distinguishing marks of the flamenco giants is the quality of their slurs. The hammers produce a powerful note, and the pull-offs have real snap to them. Often flamenco performers will go very fast with these, creating a fascinating and intricate web of sound.

Guitar Gods

John Williams, one of the greatest living classical guitarists, was born in Melbourne, Australia, on April 24, 1941. His father was also a classical guitarist, and John took his first lessons from him. He then traveled to London at the age of 11 and was taken to meet Andrés Segovia, with whom he subsequently studied.

In 1962, Williams was among the first Western guitarists to travel to the Soviet Union. He quickly proceeded to tour the United States and most of the rest of the world, where his combination of a strong classical repertoire along with a phenomenal technique soon made him a concert-hall favorite. He made three records of duets with Julian Bream, and the two toured together with great success.

Williams is one of the most prolific of all classical guitarists on record. Besides the classical repertoire, he has recorded everything from Chilean folk songs to popular works by Gershwin and Lennon and McCartney. He continues to tour regularly, spending part of each year in his native Australia.

Practice for Upward and Downward Slurs

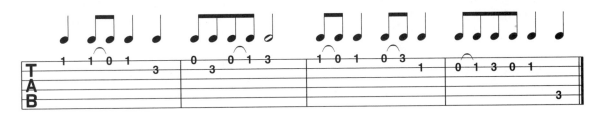

The next exercise is in flamenco style. Play the first three measures alternating *i* and *m*. In measure four, follow the marked fingering. From measure five to the end use just the thumb.

Rhythm of Soleares

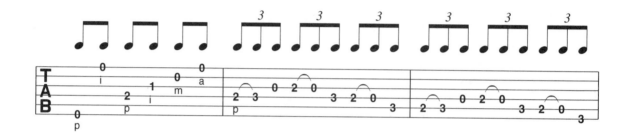

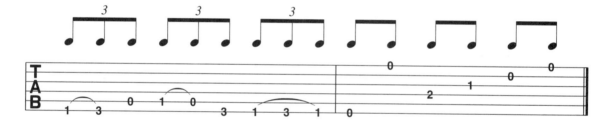

Exercise for Left-Hand Solo

Here is a challenging exercise for the left hand alone. Start by hammering on the first two notes, then pull off the next two. Then for the next group hammer the first, second, and fourth fingers and pull off to the second finger. Continue hammering on when going up in pitch, pulling off when coming down. This is excellent practice for slurs, and also for strengthening the left hand and particuarly the little finger.

The music notation is included to show which fingers are used, because in most cases the fingers do *not* coincide with the fret numbers.

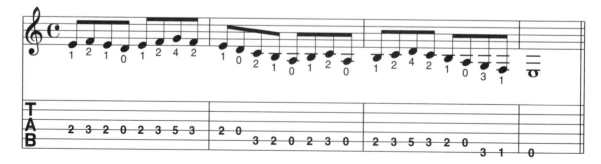

The Least You Need to Know

➤ How to do the upward slur.

➤ How to do the downward slur.

➤ How to use slurs to improve your technique and strengthen your left hand.

The Full Bar

A full bar in guitar parlance is not a crowded tavern but a valuable technique that involves placing the left-hand first finger across all the strings. This facilitates the playing of full chords that can be moved as a pattern around the fingerboard.

Learning this new skill is an important step, since it distinguishes the experienced player from the novice. If done correctly, it is an easy and comfortable device; if done wrong, it can cramp the hand and offend the ear.

In this chapter we learn to do it the right way.

Playing a Full Bar

We've seen in our previous study that the first finger of the left hand is sometimes used to cover more than one string, as in the F chord, where it is used for two strings. When the finger goes across all the strings this is known as a *full bar*. Somewhat illogically, anything less than a full bar is known as a *half bar*.

Beginners tend to find barring difficult until the left hand has acquired a degree of strength and control. However, if the bar is done correctly it is not necessary to use great strength. As with the half bar, it is far more important to find the right position for the finger so that all the notes can sound clearly with only moderate pressure.

Guitar Gods

Francisco Tárrega, the leading guitarist/composer of the second half of the nineteenth century, was born in Villareal, Spain, on November 21, 1852.

In an early recital, he is said to have played half the program on the piano and half on the guitar, then asked the audience which they preferred. When they chose the guitar, he decided to dedicate his life to the instrument. He subsequently attended the Madrid Conservatory as a student of harmony and composition, and in 1875 he was awarded first prize in these subjects.

Tárrega has deservedly been called the founder of the modern guitar school. In addition to giving concerts at home and abroad, he became a professor of guitar at the Conservatories of Madrid and Barcelona, and had a number of famous students. He established rules for the sitting position and the right hand that are followed to this day, and he also regularized the way that guitar music is written. Tárrega's tone was said by those who heard him to be unique and extraordinarily beautiful. He was a proponent of the no-nail technique, playing with just the fingertips. This was supported for awhile, particulary by his famous pupil Emilio Pujol, but the technique is now almost totally abandoned in favor of the use of the nails.

Tárrega composed over 80 original works and transcribed many more. His pieces are still played and recorded regularly.

The Full Bar

Here is how to find the right position:

1. Imagine the fret to be taller than it is, like a wall rising from the fingerboard.

2. Imagine that you are going to lay your first finger into the corner formed by that wall and the fingerboard.

3. Place the first finger across the strings at the third fret, just touching them with no pressure.

4. Little by little, ease the finger down until you make contact with the fingerboard. As you do this, pass your right-hand thumb lightly and repeatedly across the strings. At first you will hear only the deadened sound of the strings damped by the left-hand finger. Then, as the barring finger moves into its position in the "corner," the sound will become clear. At this point do *not* apply any more pressure; this is all you need.

> **Take Note**
> A full bar is defined as placing a finger of the left hand across all six strings. A half bar is placing a finger of the left hand across two, three, four, or five strings.

The other secrets to good barring are these:

➤ Make sure that the crease at the first joint of the finger does not fall on a string. Adjust the position by moving the finger forward or back until the crease lies between the third and fourth strings.

➤ Do not let the finger curve—this will produce deadened or buzzing sounds on the inside strings.

➤ Remember to make and keep contact with the fret. Stay in the "corner."

> **Key Thought**
> If your left-hand position is right, you will be surprised at how little pressure can achieve clear sounds.

As a first practical exercise start at the third fret, and try this:

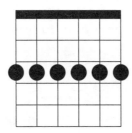

Chord block, first finger across the third fret

After playing this several times, easing into the bar until you hear a clear sound from all strings, add the notes of a full G chord like this:

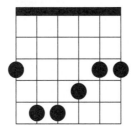

Chord block

103

This is a particularly useful chord shape, because it can be used to make a full-sounding major chord at any accessible fret on the guitar. For example:

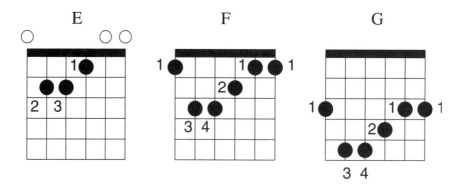

Here the E chord shape is duplicated with a bar to form other chords. In the same way, the A-minor shape may be moved to form new minor chords.

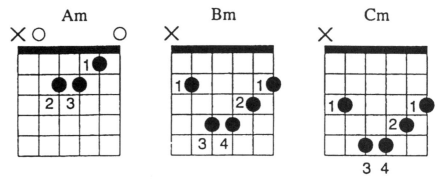

Take Note
A movable chord is defined as one that, when played in a different position, produces a new chord. Learning these patterns can help you quickly learn a wide vocabulary of chords.

Instead of showing all the frets from the beginning, it is customary to show the position on the guitar with a Roman numeral. Notes barred together are frequently shown with a slightly curved line.

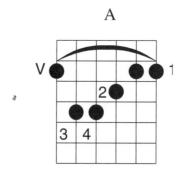

Chord block. A chord at fifth fret.

Here the A chord is played at the fifth fret with a full bar.

Now here are some more useful movable chords to add to your store.

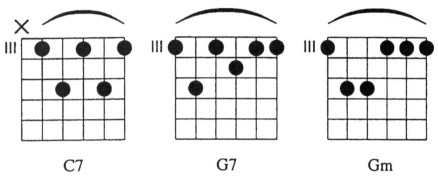

C7   G7   Gm

Movable Chords

The chords are shown with their names at the third fret. However, the G minor could be moved back to the first fret to form an F minor, or forward to the fifth fret to form an A minor.

Chord Sequences

The succession of chords needed for a piece is known as a *chord sequence*. Some sequences will work for a number of songs, for instance the much-used progression C C | Am Am | Dm Dm | G7 G7. This was affectionately known to studio musicians as "we want Cantor," a reference to the introductory music to an old radio program called *The Eddie Cantor Show*. You might try it with "Blue Moon," "Heart and Soul," or "La Mer." You will be surprised how much of these and other songs this popular sequence will fit.

Take Note
A chord sequence is a group of chords that is commonly used to accompany a melody. The very simplest one is the three-chord pattern used to accompany many folk songs.

Chord sequences are often written in simple "lead sheet" form, like this:

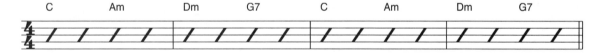

The diagonal lines (known as *hash marks*) mark the beats. Sometimes more elaborate hash marks show a specific rhythm.

Guitar Gods

Barney Kessell was born in Muskogee, Oklahoma, on October 17, 1923. Kessell began playing guitar as a youngster, working his way to the West Coast. He attracted big-band leader/comedian Chico Marx, with whom he appeared in the early forties, and from there was hired by Artie Shaw. An established presence in Los Angeles, he recorded with native and visiting musicians, including a session with Charlie Parker who was there in 1947. Kessell's smooth, cool style of playing came into vogue in the fifties, when he became a star of the West Coast jazz scene.

Kessell also worked as a studio musician, fitting in wherever he was needed. Despite his jazz background, he worked in many different styles, and can be heard on many of the pop-rock recordings cut in Hollywood in the early sixties, including the famous Beach Boys' *Pet Sounds* sessions and dozens more.

Kessell returned to jazz performance in the seventies, often touring with guitarists Charlie Byrd and Herb Ellis as the Great Guitars. His work slowed in the eighties and nineties as illness caught up with him, although he still occasionally performs.

12-bar Blues

For practice, here is the chord sequence for a typical 12-bar blues. Try using the barred chords for variety. Here's a hint: all except the E7 can be found with a bar at the fifth fret.

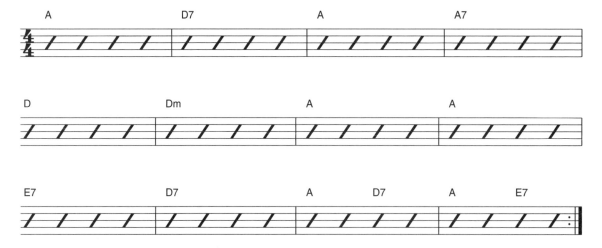

For more information on the blues, see Chapter 20.

"Dream a Little Dream of Me" (F. Andree, W. Schundt, G. Khan)

Here is a familiar song for chord practice. It was popularized in the sixties by the rock group the Mamas and the Papas, but actually it goes back decades to an earlier era of American popular song.

Let's first play the complete chords to get used to the fingerings:

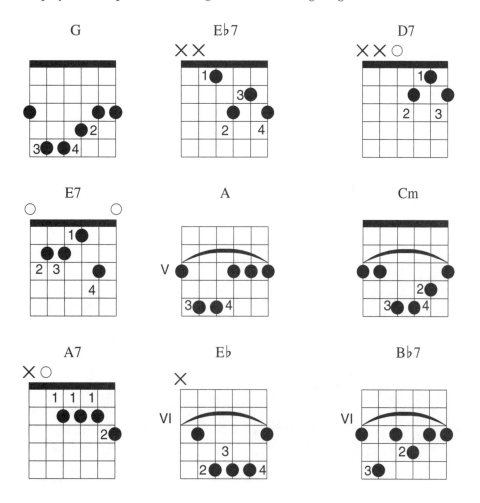

After learning the positions, try the song with a chord on each beat as indicated, using a simple sweep of either thumb or pick.

"Dream a Little Dream of Me"

Words by Gus Kahn. Music by Wilbur Schwandt and Fabiau Andree. TRO–©–Copyright 1930 (Renewed) 1931 (Renewed) Essex Music, Inc. Words and Music, Inc., New York, New York, Don Swan Publications, Miami, Florida and Gilbert Keyes, Hollywood, California

108

Additional lyrics:

Stars shining bright above you,
Night breezes seem to whisper I love you,
Birds singing in the sycamore tree,
Dream a little dream of me.

Say nightie-night and kiss me,
Just hold me tight and tell me you'll miss me,
While I'm alone and blue as can be,
Dream a little dream of me.

Bridge:

Stars fading, but I linger on, dear,
Still craving your kiss;
I'm longing to linger till dawn, dear,
Just saying this:

Chorus:

Sweet dreams till sunbeams find you,
Sweet dreams that leave our worries behind you,
But in your dreams whatever they be,
Dream a little dream of me.

Bridge

Chorus (twice)

The Least You Need to Know

➤ The full bar is an important technique that opens up many new possibilities.

➤ The secret of good barring is not using force—it is finding the right position that is important.

➤ With comparatively few bar chord patterns, you can learn a whole repertoire of new chords.

Part 4
Making Notes

Guitar tablature is fine, as long as we have music written that way. But if we want to read from "ordinary" scores or want to understand the rhythmic values of the notes, we have to learn how to read standard notation. This will be very important if we want to arrange our own guitar music. And we also have to understand a little bit of music theory: how scales are made and formed. We'll also master the advanced technique of playing more than one melody part at the same time—an integral part of classical guitar technique.

Chapter 13

How to Read Notes

In this Chapter

➤ Why learn music notation?

➤ The music staff

➤ Ledger lines

➤ Tones and half tones

➤ Hearing the octave

➤ The notes on the staff

➤ The notes on each string

So far, we've been notating (writing down) musical examples using guitar tablature, a special system of notation developed just for the guitar. Tablature is a great, easy way to learn, but it can't capture all the nuances of a piece of music. Plus, not all books feature guitar tablature.

"Standard music notation" is more common. Believe it or not, notation is not hard to learn, and once mastered it will speed your learning of new music. Any system that has survived for centuries—and is used to record all types of music—must be a valuable one to learn!

This chapter shows how music is written in standard notation for the guitar. We learn about the musical staff and how it differs from the one used for tablature. We see how notes are written on the staff and also above and below it, and we relate this to rising and falling pitch. Tones and half tones are discussed and related to the frets of the guitar. Then we put theory into practice and start actually playing from notation, with easy examples of notes on each string.

Why Learn Notation?

Pick Hit
Standard music notation evolved over centuries. Originally developed by Catholic monks to preserve church music, it quickly spread to the courts of Europe. In the 1500s and 1600s, when printed books became more common, books of printed music—both in standard notation and tablature were among the first best-sellers.

While guitar tablature is a convenient shorthand way of writing music, it is in no way a substitute for standard musical notation. Here's why:

➤ Practically everything you are going to want to learn will be in music notation. If you can only read tablature you will be confined to a very small repertoire.

➤ If you learn standard notation you can read music for any instrument. You might want to make a guitar arrangement from a piano score, or simply learn the notes of a song for which you will be working out chords.

➤ Chord construction and harmony theory is much easier to see in notation.

➤ You want to be a guitarist, but you almost certainly also want to be considered a *musician*. It is hard to achieve this if you don't understand the basic language of music. Other musicians don't read guitar tablature.

Take Note
A *score* is the printed version of a musical work.

One of the problems newcomers to music have is the difficulty of reading the time as well as the notes. Fortunately you already have experience with the basics of counting, so all we have to do now is understand how the notes fit on the music staff.

The Music Staff

The musical staff has five lines. The notes can sit on the lines or can appear in the spaces between them, like this:

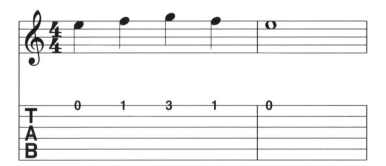

Key Thought
Remember that the lines of a musical staff represent different pitches. The lines on a guitar staff represent the different strings.

The important thing to realize from the start is that there is no similarity to the tablature staff. The lines represent musical pitch—the higher the note on the staff the higher the note. Let's examine both at once to see the correct relationship:

Notice the time signature as before, showing that the count is in quarter notes, and that there are four counts to the measure.

Play the example now, and it will be clear that the upper staff represents sounds whereas the lower (tablature) staff represents frets.

Let's try a complete melody now to see if you can relate the two.

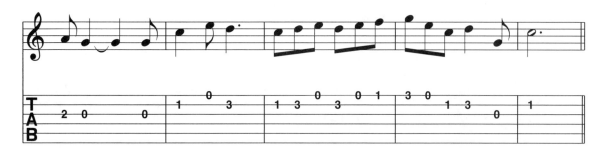

From playing the example you will have learned these points:

➤ As the notes go higher on the staff, the pitch goes higher.

➤ The measures and count are the same as for tablature.

Notes Above and Below the Staff

Obviosly there would not be enough notes with only five lines and four spaces. As a result, when extra notes are drawn above or below small lines are drawn to show their relationship to the staff. These are known as *ledger lines*.

> **Key Thought**
> A measure represents the basic metrical unit of a piece of music. In standard (4/4) time, there are four beats to a measure. The count is used to set the tempo and keep track of where you are.

Guitar Gods

Joseph Fernando Macari Sors was born in Barcelona, Spain, on February 13, 1788. He later dropped the final "s" from his last name in favor of Sor, the name by which he is commonly known. At the age of 11 he entered the excellent music school at the monastery of Montserrat, though his enthusiasm for the guitar had to remain private. At the age of 18 he wrote an opera that was produced in Barcelona, and subsequently he went to Madrid, where he enjoyed the patronage of the Duke of Medinaceli and others. During the period of French occupation, Sor chose to support the puppet government of King Joseph Bonaparte in the hope of political reform, and accepted an official appointment in Jerez de la Frontera. When the French were driven out of Spain in 1813, Sor left with them and subsequently settled in Paris. Two years later he moved to London, where he became celebrated as a performer and teacher of singing and the guitar, publishing many guitar works including his *Variations on a Theme of Mozart,* one of the most successful guitar pieces ever written. His ballet *Cendrillon,* based on the Cinderella story, was first produced at the King's Theatre in London, and went on to a tremendously successful run in Paris and further performances in Moscow.

Of all the classical "guitar gods," Sor was probably the most rounded musician, and he did much to raise the level of interest and appreciation of the instrument. His works still appear constantly on concert programs. He died in 1839.

Tones and Half Tones

Take Note
A *ledger line* is an additional line added above or below the five-line music staff to indicate higher or lower notes (falling beyond the range of the staff itself).

You may have wondered why, when notes on the music staff were placed adjacent to the tablature, they sometimes indicated a distance of one fret and sometimes two. To understand this we have to learn about *tones* and *half tones*. This is easy on the guitar, since from one fret to the next is a half tone (also called *half step* or *semitone*). A distance of two frets (i.e., from the first fret to the third) is a whole tone.

In music notation, the tones and half tones are a little harder to spot due to the way the notes are identified. Conventionally, the letters A through G are used, like this:

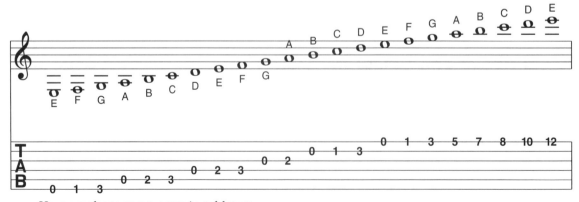

Here are those same notes in tablature.

You can see from the first three notes that E to F is only a half tone (one fret) whereas F to G is a whole tone (two frets). See if you can find the other half tone relationships.

The Octave

Now there are some things to recognize by ear. First, the interval from one note to the next one with the same letter is known as an *octave*. If you play some octaves you will notice the similarity between the upper and lower notes, and this is why the same letter is used. Try playing these:

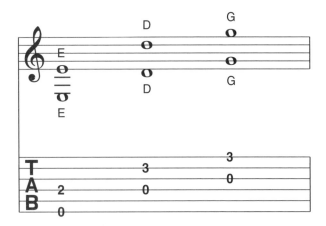

The Notes on the Staff

The names of the notes are usually memorized by separating the lines from the spaces:

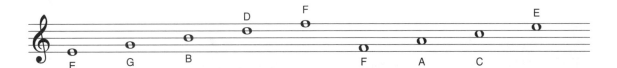

The traditional memory aid for the lines **E G B D F** is Every Good Boy Does Fine.

For the spaces, **F A C E** is easy to remember.

The Notes on Each String

Let's try reading some lines from notes alone. It won't seem difficult if we look at it string by string.

Pick Hit
The octave is a the simplest of all musical relations, 1:2. If you take a string and pluck it, it will sound a certain tone (A, for example). If you then divide the string in half and pluck it again, it will sound the *same tone*, but it will be pitched an octave higher.

Notes on the First String

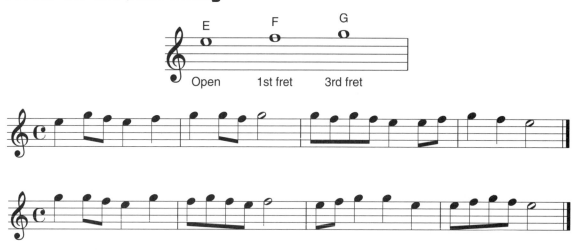

Notes on the Second String

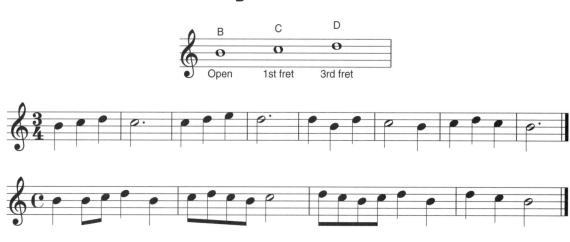

Notes on the Third String

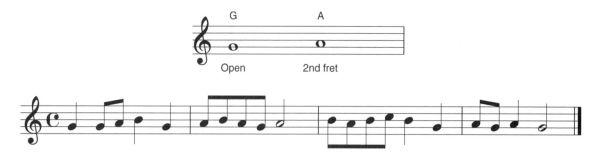

Notes on the Fourth String

Notes on the Fifth String

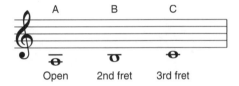

Take particular care to memorize these well. For some reason, the notes on ledger lines are harder to remember.

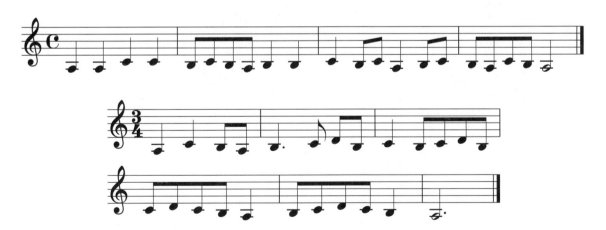

Notes on the Sixth String

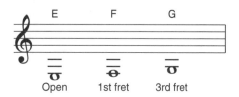

Here are some practice melodies covering all the strings.

The Least You Need to Know

➤ What a music staff looks like.

➤ The letters used for notes on the lines and spaces.

➤ How to relate tones and half tones to the guitar frets.

➤ How to read the given notes on all the strings.

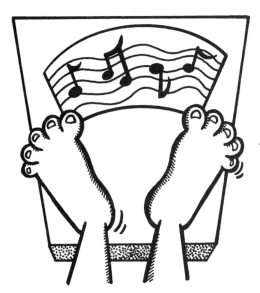

Chapter 14

The Scale

In this Chapter

➤ The C scale

➤ Sharps and flats

➤ Key signatures

➤ Simple transposing

➤ Tunes for practice

A scale is a basic building block of all music, because it forms the basis of both melody and harmony. Learning about scales will take you far along in your musical knowledge.

In Chapter 13 we learned about how the notes appear on the staff. We also learned the basic relations between the notes, as defined by half steps (the distance of one fret on the guitar) and whole steps (the distance between two frets). A scale is defined as a special relationship of half and whole steps.

In this chapter we learn that tunes are composed by selecting notes from a succesion known as a scale. We discover that a note may be raised a half step with a sharp sign (♯) or lowered with a flat sign (♭), and that this enables us to keep the same note relationships when moving a song to a higher or lower range of notes. We learn the purpose of key signatures, and how a melody may be transposed from one key to another. Finally we play some tunes from notation to put these ideas into practice.

Sharps and Flats

We now know that notes are identified for convenience by a letter name, and that the distance from one to the other may be a tone or a half tone. Why the difference? The reason is that Western music is traditionally built on certain successions of notes known as scales, the most common of which is the major scale.

Starting on the note C this is how it looks:

In the diagram, *W* stands for a whole-tone interval and *H* for a half-tone interval.

As an example, the first phrase of the tune "Bluebells of Scotland" uses all the notes of the C-major scale.

Everything works fine using the scale of C, but what happens if we want to write the tune higher or lower to make it fit our voice range? If we just shift it up the staff it won't sound right. Play it to see why:

The tune sounds different because the intervals have changed. To keep the same tune we want the interval from the second note to the third to be a half tone, as it was before. To do this we must raise the F by a half step, which we can do by inserting a sharp sign (♯).

Because we raised the pitch to use the notes of the G scale, we are now using the key of G. We find that for the tune to come out right we must raise all the Fs to F-sharp. Instead of doing this to every F individually, there is a shorthand way to do it. The sharp sign ♯ is placed at the beginning of the line on the F, showing that all Fs must be played sharp, like this:

Guitar Gods

Eric Patrick Clapton was born in Ripley, a suburb of London, on March 30, 1945. In his teenage years, he became a fan of American electric blues as played by masters like Muddy Waters and B. B. King. He began playing professionally with the Metropolis Blues Quartet in London in 1963; the group quickly changed their name to the Yardbirds, and became a successful and influential blues-revival band on the British scene.

When the band went commercial, Clapton left to join a more traditional group, John Mayall's Bluesbreakers. Soon, graffitti began appearing on London walls stating "Clapton Is God." Clapton rose even further to godlike status when he formed the first rock "power trio," Cream, along with jazz bassist Jack Bruce and drummer Ginger Baker. Clapton's soaring guitar solos became the group's trademark on everything from covers of blues standards like Robert Johnson's "Crossroads" to group originals like "Sunshine of Your Love." Still, the ever-restless Clapton avoided pigeonholing, forming another supergroup, Blind Faith, before embarking on a long and fruitful solo career. He returned to his acoustic beginnings on the hit "Tears in Heaven" (1995), inspired by the tragic death of his son, and the traditional blues album *From the Cradle* (1996).

An indication like this at the beginning of a line is known as a key signature because it helps identify the scale of notes used. It affects not only the note you see, but also those in other octaves:

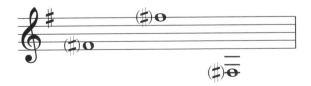

All the Fs shown would be played sharp because of the key signature.

Finally let us change the key to use the notes of the F scale. Transferring to new keys is known as transposing.

Something sounds wrong here. Can you spot what it is by playing it through? One of the notes is wrong for the tune, and in this case it needs to be lowered rather than raised a half tone.

It is in fact the B three notes from the end, and it is a half tone too high. We can lower it by putting a flat sign beside it, like this:

We can also learn from this that in the key of F all Bs are played flat, and that the key signature looks like this:

Key of F

Accidentals

Sometimes a tune departs momentarily from the key, necessitating the cancelling of what is required by the key signature. This is done by putting the required sign—sharp, flat, or natural—beside the note in question.

A natural sign (♮) means "not sharp or flat," so when we refer to A-natural we simply mean plain A, not altered by a sharp or flat.

Accidentals affect all notes until the end of the measure, after which the change is cancelled. The only exception is when a note is tied over, in which case it retains its changed status. The examples below make these rules clear.

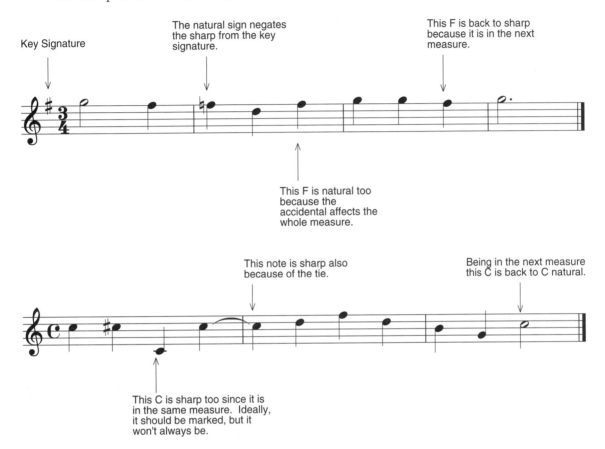

Key Signature

The natural sign negates the sharp from the key signature.

This F is back to sharp because it is in the next measure.

This F is natural too because the accidental affects the whole measure.

This note is sharp also because of the tie.

Being in the next measure this C is back to C natural.

This C is sharp too since it is in the same measure. Ideally, it should be marked, but it won't always be.

Tunes from Notation

Now that we understand the concept of sharps and flats, it is time to relate these to the guitar, and to play some tunes from notation. Here I have deliberately excluded the tablature so that you have the chance to concentrate on reading the notes.

"Plaisir d'Amour"

"Londonderry Air (Danny Boy)"

The Least You Need to Know

➤ A sharp (♯) raises the written note by a half tone. This is a distance of one fret on the guitar.

➤ A flat (♭) lowers the written note by the same amount.

➤ A natural sign (♮) negates a sharp or a flat.

➤ When written at the beginning of the musical line, sharps or flats form a key signature.

➤ When a sharp or flat is in the key signature it affects all the notes of that name in the piece.

➤ Accidentals are used to make temporary alterations to the key.

Chapter 15

Music in Multiple Voices

In this Chapter

➤ Understanding independent voices

➤ How to identify and play the parts

➤ Practical examples to count and play

➤ Three complete pieces

So far we have concentrated on reading a single line, comparable to the voice of a single singer. But from about the ninth century onward musicians have been evolving interesting ways to make music with more than one voice. Some experiments became agonizingly monotonous—for instance, when a voice was accompanied by a second voice five notes below it. This was found intolerable and was banned by theorists, and the art of counterpoint (note against note) developed, with guidelines to make the combinations work in an interesting way.

Fortunately, we can jump a thousand years by turning a page. This chapter covers reading and playing in more than one part, wiht some interesting solos to practice at the end.

Independent Voices

So far we have dealt with one musical event, be it single note or chord, happening at a time. However, music usually involves many events happening simultaneously, as when several voices sing together or different instruments play in a group. Each of the voices or instruments may be moving independently. This also happens on the guitar, where lines of music represent different "voices."

Take Note
The term *voice* or *part* refers to individual lines of music.

This is more easily understood with a practical example.

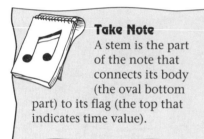

Take Note

A stem is the part of the note that connects its body (the oval bottom part) to its flag (the top that indicates time value).

Here the two separate lines or voices can be seen easily from the stem directions of the notes. How do we count two lines at once? The answer is to focus on the faster moving notes—the longer notes simply need to be held. In this example we will count three to the measure, which will give the time for the quarter notes, and simply leave the finger on the dotted half notes so that the sound continues.

Guitar Gods

John Leslie "Wes" Montgomery was born in Indianapolis, Indiana, on March 6, 1923. He had his first professional job as a guitarist playing with Lionel Hampton's big band in the late forties. In the early fifties, he formed his first trio with his two brothers—Buddy, a pianist and vibes player, and Monk, a bass player. By the late fifties, he was a successful recording artist, noted for his light touch, sweet tone, and clever reinterpretation of standards. In the sixties he virtually defined the popular jazz guitar, adapting many mainstream pop songs like "Goin' out of My Head" and "A Day in the Life" to his trio format. Montgomery became the best-selling guitarist of his day. Unlike other jazz players who played with a pick, Montgomery used his thumb to strike the strings, giving him an unusual, mellow sound. Sadly, he died in 1968, at the height of his fame.

Now try these examples.

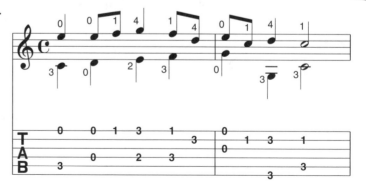

(a)   One Two and Three Four and One and Two Three Four

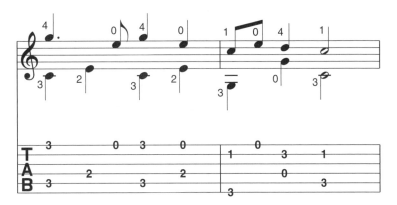

(b)   One   Two and Three Four   One and Two Three Four

Here is a piece in two voices. I have included tablature to speed up the note finding, but as far as possible try to work just from the notation in the upper line, particularly when you have tried it a few times.

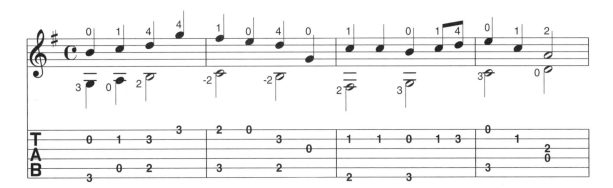

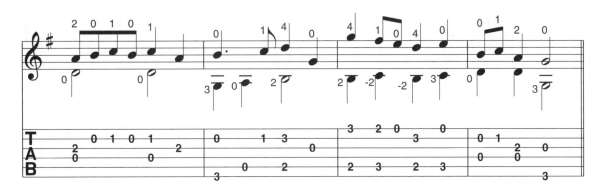

At this point we can play pieces by Sor and Bach in two parts. To give them their full effect, we need to hold the sustained longer notes, so be sure to study the notation as well as the tablature.

"Andante" (Fernando Sor)

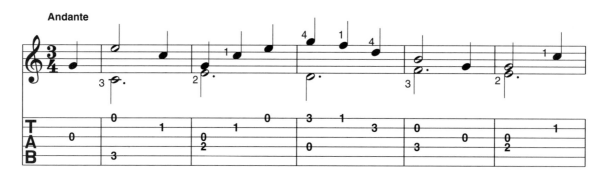

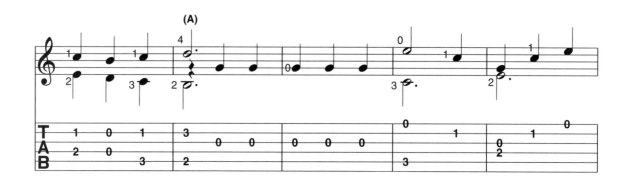

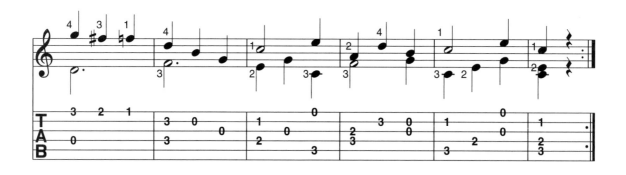

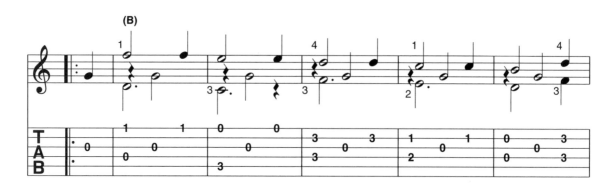

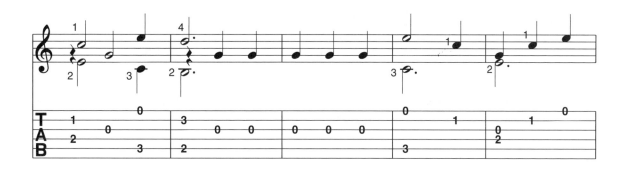

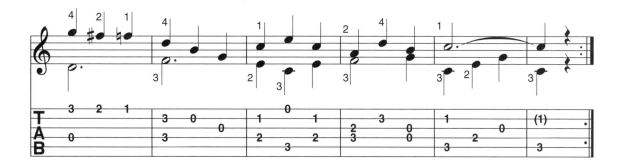

Study Notes

A. At this point, the piece actually goes into three parts, because the composer wants you to hold the D and the B for three full counts. In the following measure we are down to one voice. Sometimes this is written with rests above and below to indicate that the other parts are now silent; however, this is not necessary.

B. Here we are back in three voices again. The rest sign between the F and D at the beginning of the measure warns you that another voice is coming in the middle. The same pattern exists for the next six measures.

C. Remember to hold the high C until all the lower notes have been played.

"Bourée" (J. S. Bach)

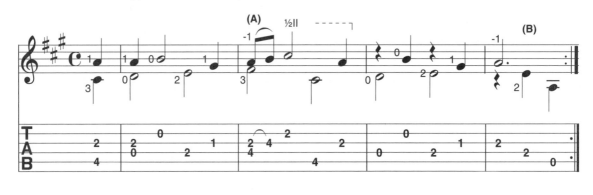

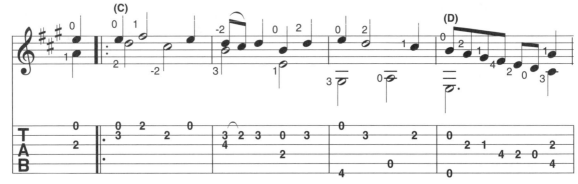

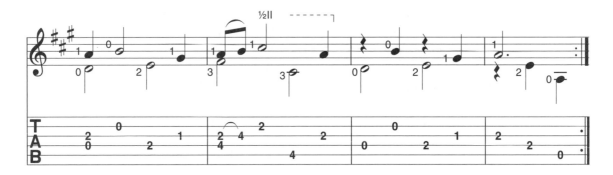

Study Notes

Although you have tablature, it is very important to follow the fingering written in the upper line because there are some necessary movements of the whole hand.

A. The small slide sign beside the first finger indicates that the finger slides up to the A. The thumb moves also so that the hand moves up into the new position.

B. The second finger crosses over to sound the E because we want the A to continue sounding and to be ready for the next measure.

C. Be sure to hold the first finger on the F-sharp in spite of the movement of the second finger.

D. This little scale passage should be practiced slowly at first. Start with the *m* finger and be sure to alternate the fingers.

"Country Dance" (Frederick Noad)

Copyright © 1968 by Frederick Noad. Used by permission.

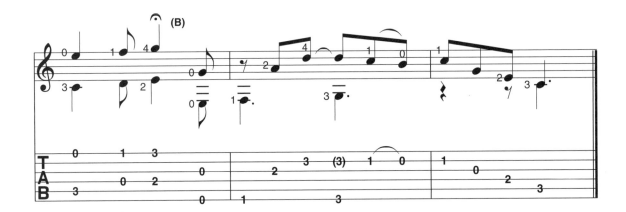

Study Notes

Practice this to a fairly brisk tempo when you know the notes. Notice that in 6/8 time there are two groups of three, so there is a feeling of two as well as of six. That is why this is known as compound time.

A. There is a slightly challenging jump of the third finger from the low G up to the F. However, if you repeat this a few times it will take the difficulty out of it.

B. The sign over the G indicates a slight hold beyond the time value. It serves to show the end of a musical phrase, and is known as a pause sign or fermata.

The Least You Need to Know

➤ How music is divided into parts, often called voices.

➤ How the different voices can be counted.

➤ How to count and play different voices at the same time, even very slowly.

Part 5
Regional Styles

All of us have our own favorite musical style, but most guitarists like to be at least conversant with different styles. You never know when you might have to accompany a hoedown or be called on to help out a Spanish dancer in need! But seriously, knowing different styles enables you to expand your technique—and eventually develop your own style. The chapters in this part of the book examine some of the most popular styles around, demystifying them and making them easy to learn.

Chapter 16

Elements of Travis Picking

In this Chapter

➤ Syncopation

➤ Some useful fingerpicking styles

➤ "Careless Love"

Once you can play and count two parts, it becomes possible to introduce a popular style of guitar accompaniment often known as Travis picking. The name is used as a tribute to Merle Travis, who popularized the style in the forties and fifties, but the roots go back to the twenties, when enterprising guitarists such as Blind Blake and Lonnie Johnson were seeking to reproduce the bounce of popular piano rags. The piano style involved a regular bass pattern against which the melody moved with dotted and off-beat notes to create a *syncopated* rhythm. The guitarists imitated this by using the thumb to imitate the piano's left hand while playing the contrasting melody with the fingers, and some achieved a considerable degree of sophistication with this technique. A famous rag by Lonnie Johnson was entitled "To Do This You Gotta Know How," and few would contest his claim.

Fingerpicking is most frequently associated with the steel-string acoustic guitar, with thumb picks helping to emphasize the bass line. However, it can be played very successfully on the Spanish guitar. Many fine singer-guitarists have favored this style including Bob Dylan, Paul Simon, James Taylor, and many, many others.

Take Note
Syncopation means the melody notes fall off the normally accented beats. Ragtime pieces, such as Scott Joplin's "Maple Leaf Rag," helped popularize syncopated rhythms.

The technique differs from standard fingerstyle in that the thumb is sometimes used on the third string when playing a repeated bass line. At the core of the style is the bouncy off-beat style known as syncopation.

Guitar Gods

Merle Travis was born in Rosewood, Kentucky, on November 29, 1917. Travis learned his unique guitar-picking style from another local player, Ike Everly, who would achieve fame through the accomplishments of his two sons, later known as rock-and-roll's Everly Brothers. Travis used a flat pick to sound the bass notes and picked the upper strings with his fingers; this unique style helped him achieve his trademark sound. His first million-selling hit was for the Los Angeles–based Capitol label, "Smoke, Smoke, Smoke that Cigarette," which he wrote with Ritter. Then, as folk music became popular, Capitol asked Travis to record some folk songs. He promptly wrote two classics, "Dark as a Dungeon" and "Sixteen Tons," both based on his father's experiences in the mines. In 1948, he worked with a local guitar maker, Paul Bigsby, to develop one of the first solid-body electric guitars; another local builder, Leo Fender, took the idea and made it into his first popular model, the Fender Telecaster. He died on October 20, 1983 in Oklahoma.

Syncopation

We expect strong beats to fall on certain beats of the bar, such as the first or third beats. We are used to them falling at least squarely on one of the beats. When they don't, a slight rhythmic hiccup develops, like this:

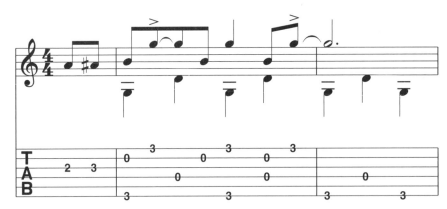

In this case, the notes with the accent marks (>) are stressed on the second half of the first and fourth beats, while the thumb bass plays squarely on the downbeat. This results in a syncopated rhythm.

To understand upbeats and downbeats, simply tap a four-beat rhythm with your fingers on a table. When the fingers go down to make the tap, that is the *downbeat*. When the fingers come up, the highest point reached marks the *upbeat*, the point halfway between the main beats. If a conductor was beating the time, his baton would travel up for the upbeat.

Here is a tune to play that includes syncopation. Notice that the "and" beats (which have accent marks) cause the syncopated effect, so give them extra stress.

> **Pick Hit**
> A famous teacher solved the problem of upbeats and downbeats by having the word "and" written on the sole of his shoe. The student sitting opposite him would see the *and* as his foot came up for the upbeat.

This type of syncopation is at the heart of the Travis picking style, where it is used to give bounce and rhythmic interest to the guitar accompaniment. Here are some examples to try using the C, F, and G7 chords:

When you play this example, let the notes ring until the chord changes. It would be more accurate to write it like this:

However, this seems a little harder to read, and the effect is exactly the same as long as the notes are held.

Now let's add more movement:

The next example adds another pair of eighth notes to each measure.

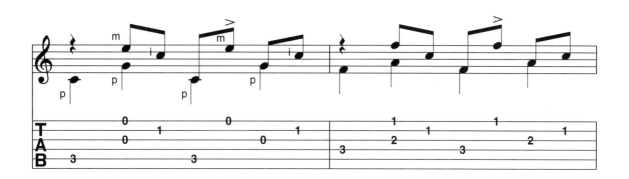

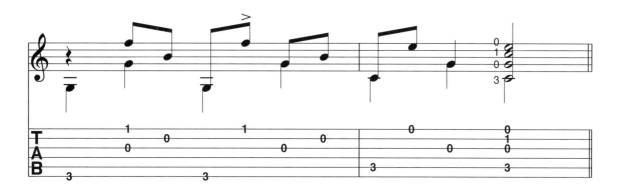

In this example, we start the movement right on the first beat for a change.

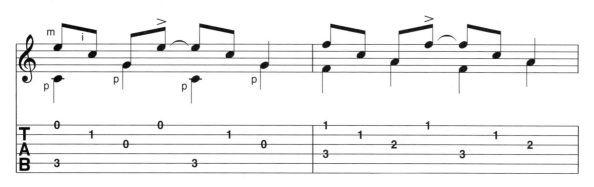

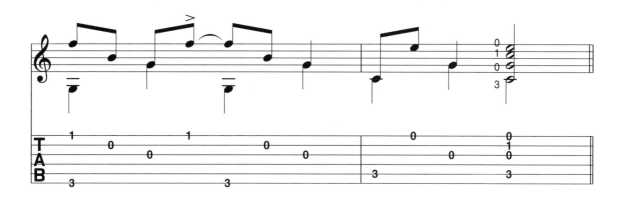

Here is a good-sounding practice example with more chord changes.

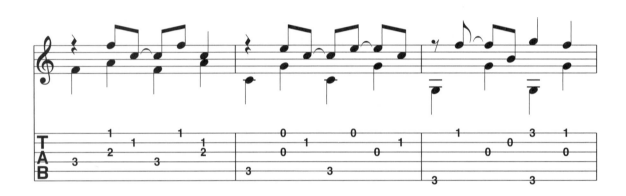

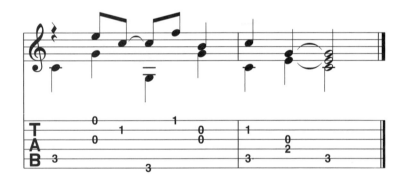

Finally, here is a complete song to try in Travis style. Notice the following points when you play it:

➤ The bass note of the chord can be alternated for variety. For example, in the first measure, instead of playing the low C twice, the low G is used.

➤ Similarly, in the second measure, the D is used as bass on the first beat instead of using the G twice.

➤ Different patterns can be mixed. For instance, the first and second measures use slightly different patterns.

➤ The real secret is to keep experimenting. Try varying both the notes of the chord and the rhythm patterns.

"Careless Love"

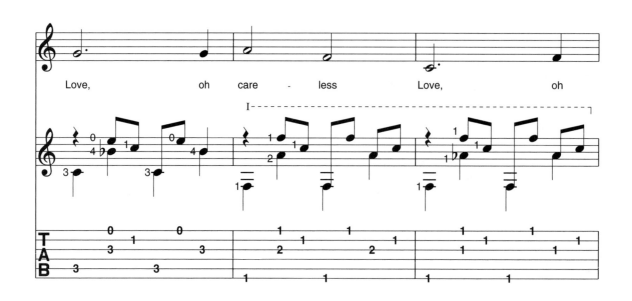

Love,   oh   care - less   Love,   oh

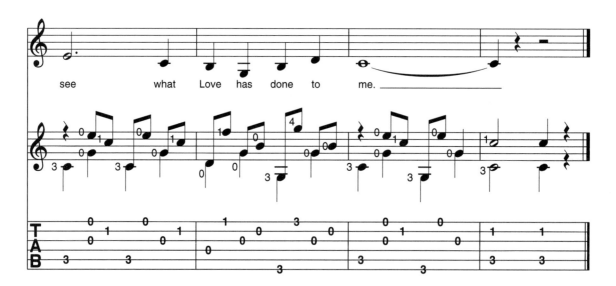

see   what   Love   has   done   to   me.

Additional lyrics:

When I wore my apron low,
When I wore my apron low,
When I wore my apron low,
You promised me you'd never go.

Now I wear my apron high,
Now I wear my apron high,
Now I wear my apron high,
You pass my door and go right by.

I love my mom and daddy too,
I love my mom and daddy too,
I love my mom and daddy too,
But I'd leave them both and go with you.

This traditional American folk song is just perfect for Travis-style accompaniment. Remember, there's no "right" way to accompany this song. Try experimenting with different bass notes and patterns until you come up with something that appeals to you.

The Least You Need to Know

➤ The term *fingerpicking* is used for a certain style of syncopated accompaniment. There are also solos in this style.

➤ The expression *Travis picking* is often used because the style was popularized by a player named Merle Travis.

➤ At the core of the style is syncopation, produced by emphasizing upbeats.

➤ Upbeats are the weaker beats that fall between the main beats of the measure. The term *upbeat* is used because the conductor's stick (or the foot of a player keeping time) comes *up* on the weak beats.

➤ You can use the Travis picking style to accompany many types of songs. By varying the bass note, you can create many unique accompaniment patterns to suit your individual taste.

Chapter 17

Folk and Country

In this Chapter

➤ Learning a simple folk accompaniment pattern
➤ Basic folk chord shapes
➤ A basic country accompaniment
➤ Playing in 3/4 time
➤ Crafting a basic solo

In Chapter 16, "Elements of Travis Picking," you learned one basic folk/country strum that is used in many playing styles. This chapter expands on that style to include some other common accompaniment techniques that will enable you to play thousands of folk and country songs.

Country music inherits an important quality, through its origin in the story songs with which Southern mountain people and their forebears in England, Scotland, and Ireland entertained themselves in the days before television. The most important element is the song. The role of musical instruments is to accompany, not to show off. You can be as fancy a guitar player in country as in any other kind of music, but what you really need to sell a country song is a good voice, good lyrics, and guitar accompaniment that doesn't get in the way.

Pick Hit
Country music alternates between periods of going back to its roots, and of having a more mainstream, cosmopolitan sound. Today's versatile country musicians use elements of every American musical style. When a country song hearkens strongly back to the original rural sound of the style, musicians ironically call it "too country for country."

Take Note

The *boom-chick strum* alternates between hitting a single bass string and a downward brush stroke across the three highest strings.

We'll begin with some simple accompaniment patterns, then progress to accompanying country songs, playing in 3/4 time, and finally crafting a traditional country solo.

A great deal of folk and country guitar playing is based on a simple accompaniment pattern. It combines picking and strumming by plucking a single bass (low) note first, followed by a downward brush stroke across the three (or so) highest strings. Usually you add variety by alternating between at least two different low notes. This is a starting point from which many more complicated variations can grow. But no matter how much fancy stuff you learn, you'll still keep coming back to this pattern. Because of the alternating high-low sound of this pattern, people often call it the *boom-chick strum.*

Keeping It Steady

Let's try this beat on a C chord. Keep your fingers down in the entire shape for a C chord. For low notes, we'll be alternating between the fifth and fourth strings.

➤ If you play with bare fingers, pluck the bass note with your thumb and make the brush stroke with your index finger. (Some people like adding one or two other fingers as well.) The idea behind using your fingers is to get a strong, bright tone from your fingernail as it sweeps across the string.

➤ If you use a flatpick, play both the individual bass note and the three note of the brush with downward strokes of a pick.

➤ If you use fingerpicks, you'll probably find them uncomfortable for making downward strokes. Use your thumbpick to play downward strokes on both the bass note and the brush.

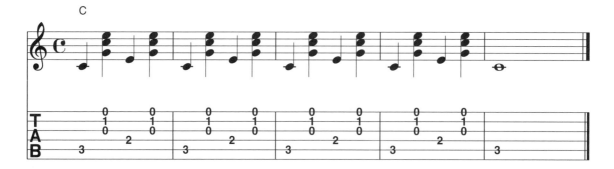

Every chord has its own alternating bass notes. On some, more than one set of alternating notes is possible. Here are diagrams of the basic chord shapes along with the alternating bass string combinations most commonly used.

Not all guitarists choose the same bass notes as their standard pattern. Almost everyone picks as the first bass note the *root* note of the chord. The root is the note the chord is named after—an A note for an A (or A-minor or A7) chord, for example. The root note is the first of the two bass notes in all the examples above. It's good to develop the habit of using the root note first. Once you get the habit down, you can start to experiment with other choices that might sound better to you at any given place in a song.

Basic Chord Shapes

The numbers indicate possible bass notes to alternate.

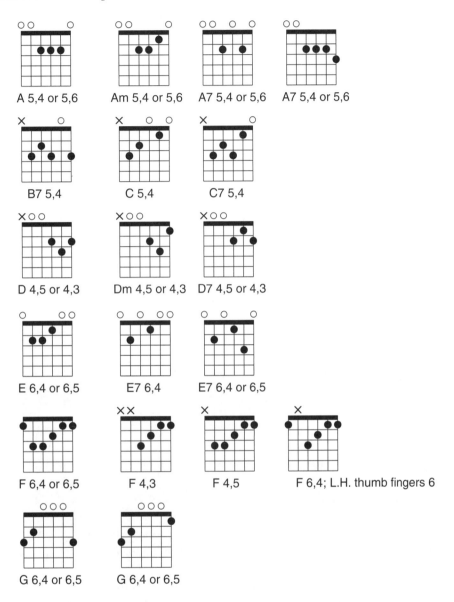

Let's practice some alternating bass notes on several chords.

Guitar Gods

Sam McGee and Maybelle Carter were important stylists in the early days of country, and rural stylist Doc Watson is highly respected for both his flatpicking and fingerpicking styles. Englishmen are among the greatest influences on modern folk guitar: Davy Graham, Martin Carthy, John Renbourn, and Richard Thompson, along with Frenchman Pierre Bensusan. They extended traditional guitar techniques, adding new influences from a variety of styles and bringing them to bear on new age, Celtic, and contemporary folk and pop sounds. Clarence White, Tony Rice, and Charles Sawtelle developed the voice of the guitar in bluegrass, the country cousin of country music. Country singers usually just strum, but Ricky Skaggs, Vince Gill, and Willie Nelson are among today's stars who are also fine pickers. Country music has produced few solo guitar careers like that of Chet Atkins because it is a vocally oriented music. Many of the most respected players are band musicians, and names like Roy Nichols (with Merle Haggard) and Don Potter (with the Judds) come quickly to mind. Even virtuosos like the late Danny Gatton spend much of their career as team players. The true guitar heroes in Nashville are the recording session players whose names you see in small print on the back of the CD booklet—if at all. Listen between the lines to the way the entire band works together to complement the singer, build the arrangement, and bring out the meaning of the song.

Picking a Country Song

Now we can move on to a favorite folk, country, and bluegrass song to accompany with this pattern. Although all the notes in the accompaniment part are written out to guide you, the most important thing is to keep the beat going. Don't worry if sometimes you don't exactly brush exactly the three strings that are indicated, just as long it sounds like a good, ringing strum. Aim at getting more accurate with more experience.

Playing a Solo: "Will the Circle Be Unbroken?"

The words and vocal melody to "Will the Circle Be Unbroken?" are given below, in addition to the guitar accompaniment. If you want, you and a friend can learn to play both parts on the guitar, and switch off playing lead and accompaniment.

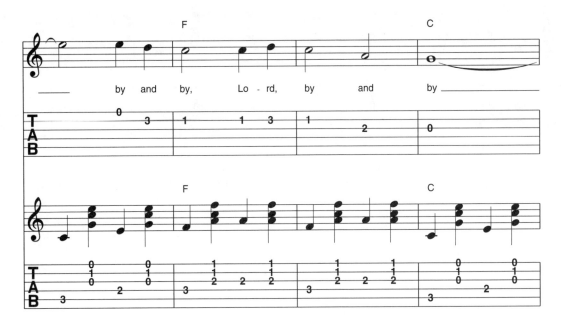

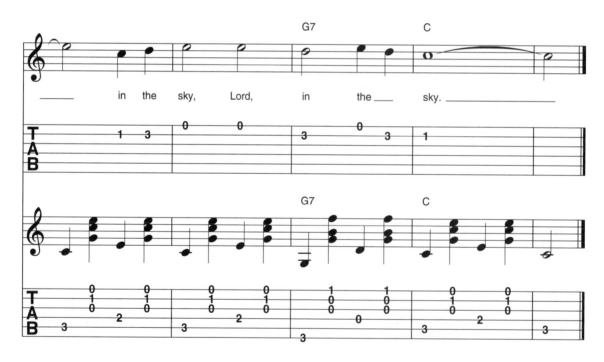

When you encounter a song in 3/4 time, you'll need to adapt the pattern to work in units of three. *Bass brush* has two components. To get the feeling of three beats, just add one more brush.

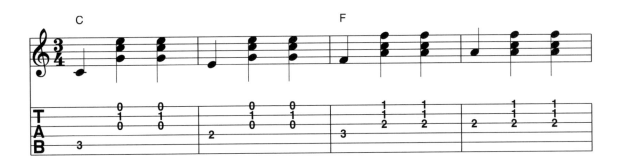

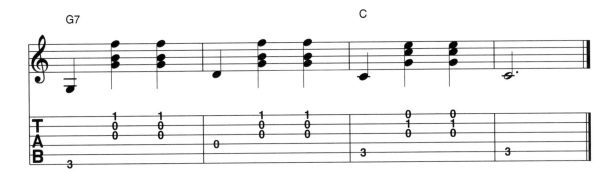

Make it your business to learn to accompany about a zillion songs with these patterns. Ideally, you should become perfectly comfortable with it before moving on to anything else. But just to give you a little taste of how this pattern can be developed, let's use it to play the melody of "Will the Circle Be Unbroken?" We'll do this by playing the melody notes instead of the ordinary bass notes.

As you follow the music you'll see that sometimes you need to move or add a finger to play a melody note that is not one of the notes of the chord, but keep the chord shape in place as much as you can and always get back to it. You'll notice that you really have to move some fingers around on the F chord. From the chord chart earlier in the chapter, choose one of the F chord shapes that doesn't use the complete bar, so you can get to the open strings when you need them.

Key Thought
It's easiest to find the melodies of most folk and country songs in the keys of C, G, A minor, and E minor. Other keys are more challenging because they use chords with shapes that make it harder for your fingers to get to the melody notes and still have enough of the chord shape left to strum on.

Also notice how every now and then a bass note is used in the spot where there would normally be a brush. This is something you sometimes have to do in order to get the melody out clearly. Some melodies are so busy that, in order to get them out, you'd hardly find time to brush at all. Songs like this are not well suited to this style of playing.

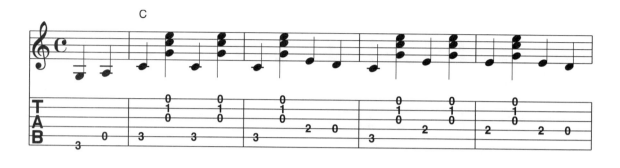

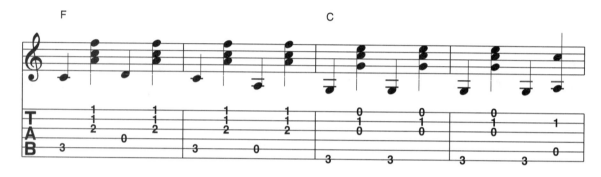

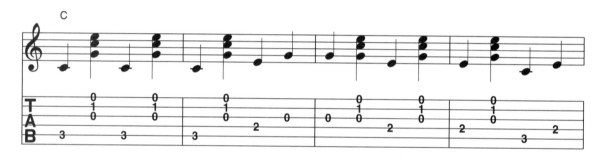

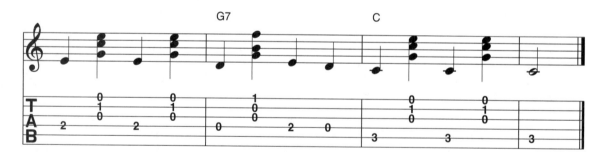

The Least You Need to Know

➤ Folk and country guitar skills are based on physical gestures like chord shapes and rhythmic picking and strumming patterns. Idiomatic guitar playing in these styles depends more on using these gestures as building blocks than on reading notes.

➤ The *bass-note brush* accompaniment is an important building block. Learn to use it comfortably and it can take you a long way beyond the music in this chapter.

➤ The important thing in folk and country music is to *sell the song* by performing it well. Careers as flashy soloists in this style are limited. If your goal is to be strictly an instrumentalist, you may find greater musical and career satisfaction if you concentrate more on supporting singers and learning band teamwork than on egotistical soloing.

Pick Hit

Picking out melody notes in the bass, accompanied by brushing the high strings in between, is often called *Carter* style because it was popularized by Maybelle Carter of the pioneer country group the Carter Family. The Carters began a musical dynasty. June Carter Cash was a member of the second generation and Rosanne Cash and Carlene Carter are part of the current generation.

Introducing Flamenco

In this Chapter

➤ What is flamenco?

➤ Development of the solo art

➤ The flamenco forms

➤ Right-hand technique

➤ The flamenco downstroke

➤ The upstroke

➤ The downward *rasgueo*

➤ The down and up *rasgueo*

➤ *Soleares*

➤ *Farruca*

When many people think of the guitar, they think of the dramatic folk music of southern Spain known as *flamenco*. This passionate music is closest to the heart and soul of the Spanish guitar, and every guitarist will be tempted to learn at least one flamenco piece.

Flamenco is the music of the gypsies of Andalusia, with origins that draw on the musical tradition of the Moors and Sephardic Jews as well as that of the gypsies themselves. In the early part of the nineteenth century, this music found popularity with a wider audience through its presentation in the *café cantante,* a place for enthusiasts to gather and hear what was previously the music of the campfire.

Like the blues in America, flamenco acquired a following among privileged groups of people far removed from the suffering and deprivation that gave birth to many of the songs. These songs that cry from the heart are the essence of flamenco, and the guitar, now as then, is the favored instrument of accompaniment.

The Flamenco Forms

Take Note

Cante is Spanish for "song." *Cante jondo* or *cante hondo* literally means "deep song."

There are more than 30 different groups of flamenco songs, relating to different regions and occupations, from the *martinete* of Triana performed to the sound of a blacksmith's hammer striking an anvil to the *tarantas* and *mineras* of the mining communities of the southeast. The songs are broadly divided into two categories: *cante jondo*, the serious forms, and *cante chico*, the more lighthearted type.

For the student, the most popular forms to study are the *alegrías,* played in A to accompany the dance and in E as a solo; the *soleares,* inspiration for many great *falsetas;* and the *seguiryas* with its fascinating rhythm which alternates measures of 3/4 and 6/8.

Take Note

Falsetas are improvised melodic passages added to the end of a vocal line by the flamenco guitarist to add to the mood of the performance.

Popular also are the various local forms of the *fandango,* known in Malaga as *Malagueñas* or in Granada as *Granaínas,* and from the Atlantic coast the ever popular and lively *fandangos de Huelva*. Also well known is the dramatic dance known as the *farruca,* a feature of José Greco's worldwide tours.

Development of the Solo Art

As an outgrowth of early flamenco, in which the guitar was confined strictly to an accompaniment role, a solo guitar art developed, pioneered by the legendary Ramón Montoya. In accompanying the songs, the guitarist usually plays plain chords during the verses. However, at the end of the verse, giving the singer time to draw breath, the guitarist plays a variation which shows his skill and adds to the mood. These interludes were known as *falsetas,* and the solo repertoire grew from the piecing together of a number of *falsetas* with lengthier and more fanciful elaborations.

Guitar Gods

Ramón Montoya, a legendary flamenco performer and innovator, was born on November 2, 1880. Although much in demand as an accompanist by artists such as Antonio Chacon and the great dancer "La Argentinita," Montoya is equally celebrated for his development of a solo style. His *falsetas* have been imitated by every subequent generation of guitarists, and his innovations included entirely new solo forms such as the *rondeña.* A solo record made for Chant du Monde in Paris has become a rare collector's item, as has Montoya's record with Manolo de Huelva (Dial Discos 54 9317–19). The latter was considered by many to Montoya's equal, but he was more secretive about his atristry and thus made less of an impact on the world of flamenco guitar.

Ramón's nephew, Carlos Montoya, is reputed to have been unsuccessful in seeking lessons from the great man. However, Carlos persisted with the guitar and toured with a number of famous artists. He settled in the United States in 1940, where his theatrical presentations did much to popularize the flamenco guitar.

In this century, flamenco has grown and flourished with innovations of style and harmony and guitarists of phenomenal technique. The wizardry of Paco de Lucia, Habichuela, and Tomatito has to be heard to be believed. Paco Peña has, in addition to his own innovations, reproduced the classic performances of Niño Ricardo and Ramón Montoya.

Technique

Usually flamenco is not written down, being passed by listening and memorization from player to player. However, it is possible to learn some of the basics of flamenco technique provided that this is backed up with much listening to good players and singers.

Flamenco technique is broadly divided into two categories—*rasgueado* (literally, scraped) and *picado* (picked). The *rasgueado* is used to establish rhythms with percussive strokes and strums of the right hand. This is particularly important when accompanying dancers, where the guitar needs to be audible above the sound of song and stamping feet.

The *picado* (plucked) technique is similar to normal fingerstyle playing, and is used for the *falsetas*. In flamenco, there is emphasis on the clean playing of scales and arpeggios, and in fact a high level of right-hand skill is expected. The tremolo (see Chapter 21) is also used, though purists tend to discourage excessive use of this technique.

Flamenco players frequently use a capo, in fact it is rare to see the guitar used without one. The most commonly used postion is at the second fret, but higher postions are sometimes used. The raised pitch adds brightness to the sound, which helps audibility when singers and dancers are involved.

> **Pick Hit**
> One reason why cypress wood is traditionally used for flamenco guitars is to ensure that they can be heard over the noise of the crowds. The resulting tone is more metallic than other woods, and this tends to cut through better.

> **Take Note**
> A *capo* is a device that is used to raise the pitch of a guitar. By placing a capo across the strings at the second fret, for example, the player can finger a "C" chord but will actually play a "D" chord.

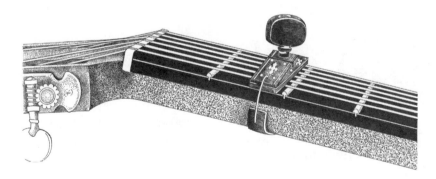

The flamenco capo

Right-Hand Techniques

The Flamenco Downstroke

The first step in training the right hand is an easy one. The index finger strikes down to sound a chord with the back of the nail, like this:

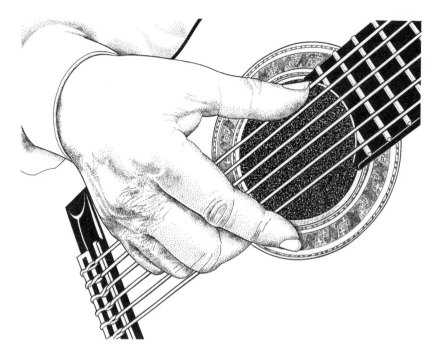

The flamenco downstroke

In notation this is often shown with a downward arrow:

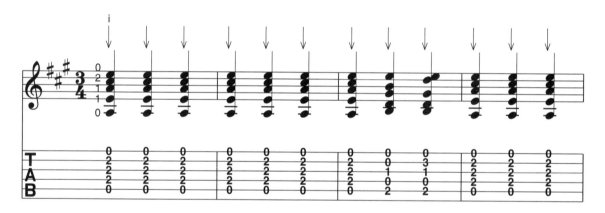

Key Thought

If great emphasis or volume are required, the other fingers may be used together with the index finger, but it is best at first to practice with the index alone.

Play this now, trying to make make as close to a single sound as possible. There is no scrape involved in the downstroke, which is used to establish the fundamental beat.

Notice the typical flamenco fingering of the A chord. The first finger covers both the fourth and third strings, leaving two other fingers available for added notes and for damping.

Damping

The downstroke may be allowed to ring, but sometimes the sound is cut off to accentuate the rhythm. The sound is deadened, or *damped*, in various ways. With the right hand, the fingers may simply be replaced on the strings after playing a chord. If the chord was played with the thumb, the side of the hand may be easily used to stop the sound. If the chord was played fingerstyle, i.e., with thumb and fingers, then it is sufficient simply to put them back on the strings as if preparing another chord.

Take Note
To *damp* a note is to deaden or cut it off, so that it does not continue to sound or ring.

Flamenco Damping

As already explained, the A chord is fingered using the just the first and second fingers. This leaves the little finger free, which is frequently used to cut the sound of a chord. Try playing the example again, and after each chord let the little finger touch the strings to stop the sound. The finger is straight so as to reach across all the strings.

Skilled flamenco performers can play fast successions of chords, each of which is clearly and crisply defined by this method.

The Upstroke

An upstroke with the index finger is frequently added to the downstroke when a faster tempo is desired. Like the downstroke, it should not drag across the strings, the aim being for clear-sounding chords. In notation this would be shown with an upward arrow. The notation is simplified with a chord symbol because many repeated chords tend to look unnecessarily complicated. Do the upstrokes and downstrokes as indicated by the arrows.

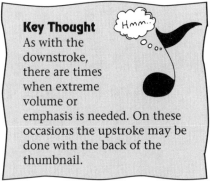

Key Thought
As with the downstroke, there are times when extreme volume or emphasis is needed. On these occasions the upstroke may be done with the back of the thumbnail.

The flamenco upstroke

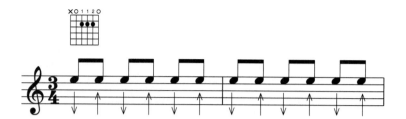

Try this example with an even count of one-and two-and three-and. You will find it helps to rest the thumb on the bottom string to stabilize the hand.

Now try mixing the two types of stroke in this pattern:

The Rhythmic Tap (Golpe)

The dances of Spain and Latin American make frequent use of percussive sounds to accentuate the rhythm. The flamenco guitar is protected with a tap plate for this purpose, either white or transparent, glued to the face of the guitar. Often the downstroke is accentuated with a simultaneous *golpe*. As the index finger moves across the strings the ring finger moves sharply down onto the tap plate.

A number of flamenco forms have rhythmic groups of 12 beats, as shown above. This pattern is known as the *rhythm of bulerías*. Unlike conventional Western music that would stress the first of each group of three, the flamenco stresses are commonly on 3, 6, 8, and 10, with 11 and 12 being weak beats.

The Rasgueo

Downward Rasgueo

Key Thought
The *rasgueo* is the characteristic flamenco stroke pattern that gives the music its unique sound.

Now we come the *rasgueo* itself. Instead of just the index finger we are going to do a downstroke with the three fingers *a*, *m*, and *i*.

As you strike the strings, try to make distinct sounds—it is not a miscellaneous scrape but three separate events.

To make this clear, first count this line to feel the rhythm:

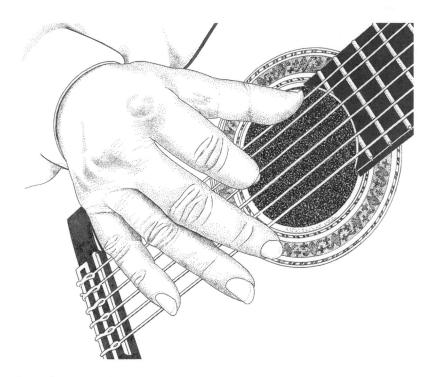

The fingers go down in succession

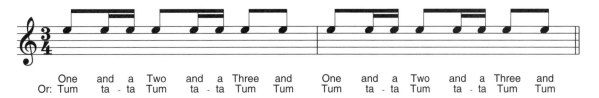

| One | and | a | Two | and | a | Three | and | One | and | a | Two | and | a | Three | and |
| Or: Tum | ta | - ta | Tum | ta | - ta | Tum | Tum | Tum | ta | - ta | Tum | ta | - ta | Tum | Tum |

It is easier sometimes to make word syllables like this that express the rhythm.

The next step is to prepare the left hand with a complete E chord, and to play the downstrokes for each finger as indicated.

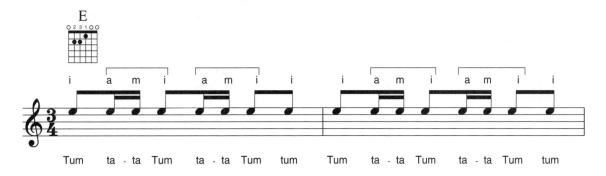

I have not included arrows because all strokes are downward.

Notice that the three fingers moving down time with the "ta-ta tum." The other chords are simple downstrokes.

Guitar Gods

Sabicas, one of the great innovators of solo flamenco performance, was born in Pamplona, Spain, on March 15, 1912. With an amazingly strong and accurate technique, Sabicas was a dazzling performer although, his stage presentation was restrained and concentrated rather than flashy. He toured with Carmen Amaya, José Greco, and others but in later life he focused on solo performance. In this area, he introduced some harmonic developments and created marvelous solos out of less familiar forms such as the *garrotin.* He lived for many years in New York, where he died in 1990. Since his death, there has been a great revival of interest in Sabicas's records, which are now eagerly sought by collectors on both sides of the Atlantic.

Developing the Fingers

It is important to practice the *rasgueo* pattern extensively. At first the fingers will tend to scrape down together, because the ring finger, *a,* doesn't want to separate from the middle finger. Then, with practice, it becomes possible to get three clear sounds.

To unlock the ring finger, there is an excellent exercise for developing dexterity and independence.

➤ In a sitting position, place your right hand above your right knee. Make a fist.

➤ Flick out the little finger.

➤ Now flick out the ring finger. This is the hard one.

➤ Finally flick out the middle and then the index fingers.

Four-Finger Rasgueo

Now comes the four-finger *rasgueo,* starting with the little finger. I have used the letter *l* for this finger. After thorough practice of the three finger pattern, this will seem easier. However, without the prior work to free the ring finger, it becomes a meaningless scrape. Following the example above (rhythm of *Malgueñas*), we have a triplet instead of the two sixteenth notes. Expressed in words, *tum ta-ta tum ta-ta tum* becomes *tum tiddly tum tiddly tum.* The four downward strokes time to the *tiddly tum.* It is still important to try for clear sounds. Here it is in notation:

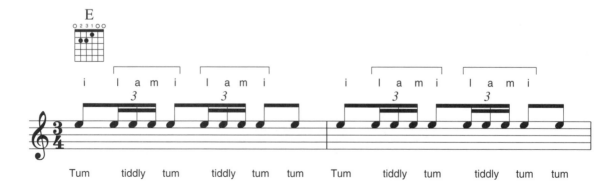

As before, all strokes are in a downward direction.

Once you can play this, try the *Malagueña* study that follows. I have simplified the notation in the same way.

Study Note

Although most of this study is *rasgueado,* there are some short segments of single notes *(punteado).* For simplicity, I have marked these with a *v* mark over the notes. Try to keep the count of three going throughout.

   A. Here is the first segment of single notes marked with *v.*

Down and Up Rasgueo

After practicing the downward *rasgueo* and working on separating the fingers, it becomes possible to learn a form of *rasgueo* that is perhaps the most important—the one that involves an immediate upstroke following the downward movement of the fingers.

The *rasgueo* for *Malagueñas* started on a weak beat and ended on a strong one. Like the di-di-di-*da* which forms the letter "V" in Morse code, the *l, i,* and *m* fingers were followed by the index finger on a strong beat. In contrast, the *rasgueo* that we are about to learn starts on a downbeat. Here is how it would look in notation:

The important thing is that the four strokes, three down and one up, are evenly spaced with a slight extra stress on the first ring finger downstroke. You can try it first away from the guitar so as to have it clearly in mind. Here are the steps:

   ➤ In a sitting position place your right hand above your right knee. Make a fist.
   ➤ Flick out the ring finger.
   ➤ Now flick out the middle finger.
   ➤ Flick out the index finger.
   ➤ Pull the index finger back toward you.

The timing should be an even *one*-two-three-four with a slight extra push on the one.

It becomes apparent now why it was necessary to prepare the fingers with the *Malagueña rasgueo.* The all-important secret is to develop the ability to do the ring finger downstroke separated from the middle finger. It is hard at first, but comes with practice.

Now let's try it on the guitar. The *rasgueo* is followed by simple upstrokes and downstrokes, keeping a regular rhythm.

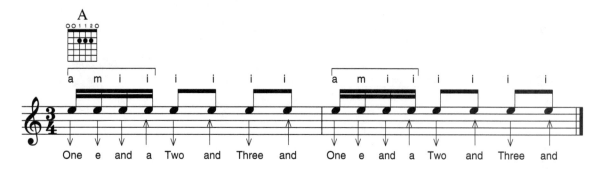

Before playing, count out the rhythm as above. Then try playing the pattern, making the individual strokes as clear as possible. Then, as your tempo increases, you will develop the even sound of a good *rasgueo*.

For practice, here are some typical introductory *rasgueado* sequences.

Rhythm of Soleares

The *soleares* is one of the best known flamenco forms. It is a serious form, but a fast version of it developed into the popular *bulerías,* a humorous gypsy dance involving clowning gestures and steps.

Here is a *soleares* introduction, followed by typical *falsetas.* The 12 beats of the *rasgueado* segment are normally accented on 3, 6, 8, and 10, and the 11 and 12 beats are weak or silent.

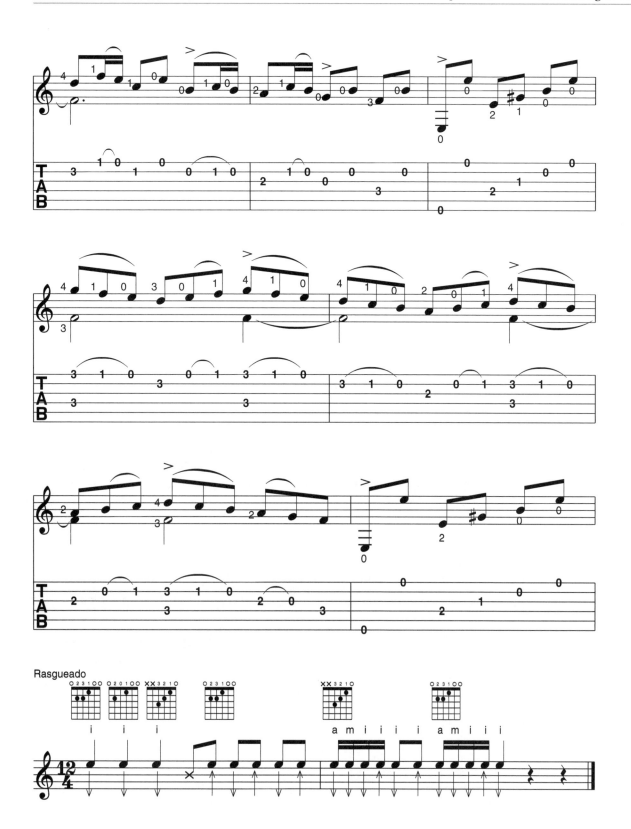

Rasgueado

Study Notes, Soleares

    A. In the opening *rasgueado,* written in 12/4, remember to stress 3, 6, 8, and 10.

    B. The *falsetas* are written in 3/4 because it is easier to read and understand this way, even though there is still a feeling of 12. Observe the accent where marked by the symbol >.

Farruca

The *farruca* alternates between A minor and E7 harmony, with *falsetas* separating the rhythm passages.

Study Notes, Farruca

    A. For simplicity, I have shown the chords in blocks. You may wish to practice the *rasgueado* first on a single chord, then make the changes. Note that the first line is played twice.

    B. The first four notes of the *falseta* are slurred. Play the first note with the thumb, hammer the second note, and pull off the remaining two. It sounds difficult but it actually does make it easier.

    C. All four notes are slurred here. Play the first, hammer the second, and pull off the remaining two. Try to keep them even as written.

    D. Finger the D minor chord 0,2,3,1, instead of the more usual 0,2,4,1. Then for the chord at the beginning of the next measure simply, add the little finger on the G and take it off for the following chord.

    E. This sign indicates a *golpe* or tap. If you do not have a plastic tap plate on your guitar, I suggest using the fleshy side of the thumb for the percussive sound in order not to damage the face of your guitar.

Farruca

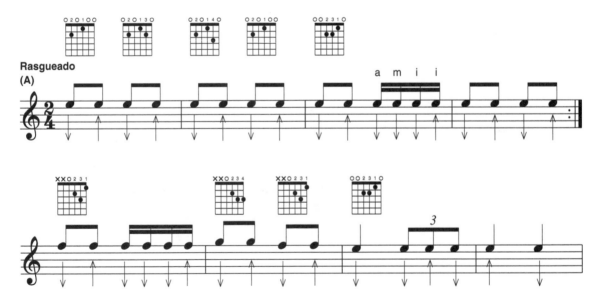

Falseta 1
(B)

(C)

gradually increase speed

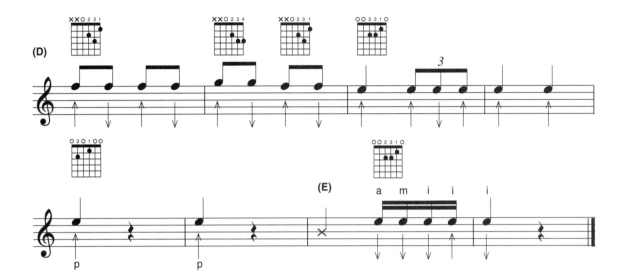

The Least You Need to Know

➤ Flamenco is the music of Andalusia in southern Spain.

➤ The strumming used to mark the rhythms is known as *rasgueado*.

➤ Between the strummed rhythms come improvised melodic passages known as *falsetas*.

➤ The rhythmic tapping to mark the beat is known as *golpe*.

➤ Putting all these elements together takes time and practice, but the result is an authentic flamenco style!

Chapter 19

Latin Rhythms

In this Chapter

➤ Tango

➤ Rumba

➤ Beguine

➤ Bossa nova

➤ *Carnavalitos*

The guitar and the vihuela were carried to the New World by the Spaniards and the Portuguese, and a host of new forms and rhythm patterns developed. In this chapter, we try playing some of these forms, and practice shaping the rhythms with accented upbeats and damping. We play the tango, the rumba, and the beguine, and then learn some typical chords to practice the bossa nova. Finally we learn a solo, a popular dance form from Peru known as *carnavalitos*.

Tango

An ever popular dance is the tango, with its distinctively clipped sound.

Starting on a stressed upbeat, the count is:

and One Two Three Four **and One** Two Three Four, etc.

Take Note
The Argentinian tango was popularized in the United States beginning in the early twentieth century by performing dancers like Vernon and Irene Castle. It is a syncopated dance, like ragtime, but with stronger accents on the introductory upbeat.

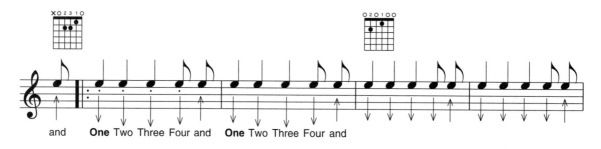

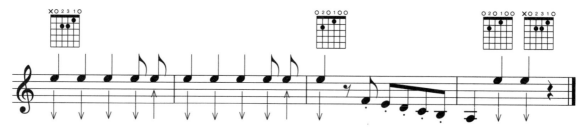

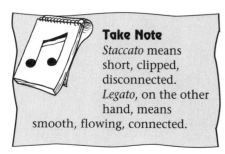

Take Note

Staccato means short, clipped, disconnected. *Legato*, on the other hand, means smooth, flowing, connected.

Pick Hit

The rumba was popularized in the thirties and forties by Cuban bands such as the ever-popular Xavier Cugat and Desi Arnaz (later the costar of the *I Love Lucy* television show).

The quarter note chords have been marked with a *staccato* sign marked in the first measure, indicated by the dots below the notes. This means that the chords should be cut off by damping, in this case with the left hand little finger, to give them the dramatic effect typical of this form.

This does not apply to the upbeat eighth note chords which, by contrast, should last their full value, giving a tar-*rump* effect. The staccato on the single notes shortens the time they are held, but each note starts on its beat as written, i.e, the overall tempo is not changed. The notes simply have a clipped sound.

As with all the forms illustrated here, there are many variants, but once you understand the basic rhythm you will be able to experiment with making variations.

Rumba

Another popular dance style that came to these shores from Cuba is the rumba. It has its own specific, syncopated style. It starts on the downbeat with a stress on the second half of the second beat.

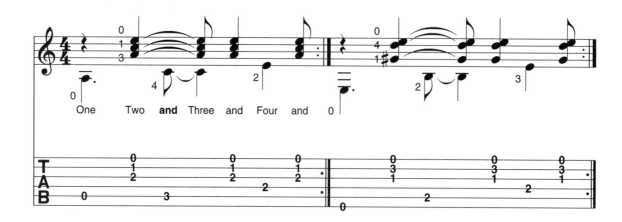

The Beguine

For the beguine, the stressed upbeat comes at the beginning:

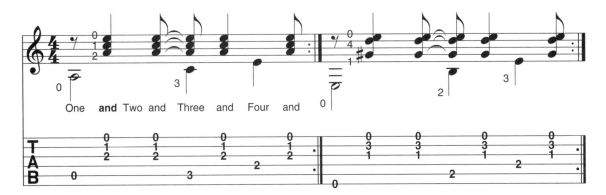

The Bossa Nova

The bossa nova from Brazil has an intriguing mixture of jazz chords and Latin rhythm. To get the feel of this on the guitar, it is first necessary to learn some chords before concentrating on the rhythmic structure. Below, for instance, is a very typical sequence, not too hard to play because of the way that the second, first, and third fingers progress down the fingerboard. After the first four chords you can still slide the second and third fingers, adding the fourth finger on the second string. Then if you lift the second finger you have the final one of the group, ready to repeat back to the first. Here we go:

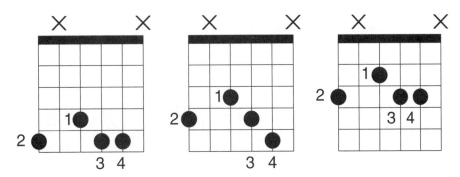

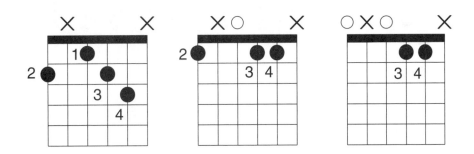

Guitar Gods

Laurindo Almeida, one of the most influential guitarists on the North American scene, was born on September 2, 1917, in São Paulo, Brazil. After a radio debut at the age of 15, he gave concerts in Brazil's major cities. After crossing the Atlantic as a musician on the liner *Cuyaba,* he heard Django Reinhardt play in Paris, an experience that changed his whole attitude to music.

After World War II Almeida relocated to the United States and became an important member of the Stan Kenton orchestra. In the sixties he was one of the first to introduce the Brazilian bossa-nova sound. He led a quartet with saxophonist Bud Shank, and together they made a number of highly successful records for the Pacifica label. In addition, he recorded many classical guitar works, including the debut recording of Heitor Villa-Lobos's guitar concerto. Later in his life, Almeida gave recitals with his wife, soprano Delta Eamon. A musician of extraordinary versatility, he composed more than 200 works. His death in 1996 was a great loss to the guitar world.

When you feel comfortable with the chords, try playing the sequence in this rhythm:

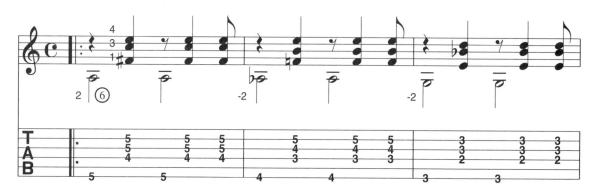

I suggest playing each measure twice at first to focus on the right hand. Giving the slight extra weight to the upbeat after the third count is what establishes the correct feel. There is also a languid feel which is best learned by listening to good players.

Carnavalitos

Here is a complete solo in Peruvian style, the *carnavalitos*. The basic rhythm is:

This rhythm is played with many variants. Try to play it in a rhythmic and sprightly way, thinking of a dance at carnival time. This piece should present few difficulties, but be sure to accent the notes marked with the symbol >.

The Least You Need to Know

➤ Latin and Spanish rhythms have long been popular in the United States.

➤ Dance forms such as the tango, rumba, beguine, and particularly bossa nova have blended with U.S. styles.

➤ The blend of jazz and bossa nova during the sixties was highly influential on guitarists.

➤ It's easy and fun to play these Latin rhythms!

> **Pick Hit**
> Agustín Barrios (1885–1944) was a Paraguayan virtuoso of the guitar who also composed extensively, though much of his fine music remained in obscurity until recent times. To add panache to his concerts, Barrios would wear a feathered Indian headdress; he later adopted the name of Mangoré, a legendary chieftain.

Carnavalitos

Chapter 20

The Blues

In this Chapter

➤ What are the blues?

➤ Introducing the 12-bar blues

➤ Building a blues solo

➤ A complete blues instrumental

Recently, performers like Eric Clapton have been returning to their acoustic origins and have started once again to play in a blues style. The screaming guitar sounds of the electric blues have become an indelible part of our music. Before that, there was the quieter though no less powerful blues of the acoustic guitar, played on front porches and at backwoods gatherings by itinerant musicians for whom sung lyrics were just as important as their inventive guitar parts.

The blues began as a folkloric music in rural African-American communities in the last decades of the nineteenth century. By the twenties, the style was perfected by specialized singer-songwriter-guitarists. But blues was also performed by songsters like Leadbelly and Henry Thomas, who also sang story songs, children's songs, comic songs, and even spirituals. The blues was also quickly assimilated by early jazz and rural dance bands and even Tin Pan Alley.

This chapter teaches you the basics of the blues: from the fundamental underlying 12-bar pattern that fits thousands of songs, to learning blues chords, and then finally mastering a blues instrumental.

Pick Hit

Singing the blues wasn't always as bad as it's cracked up to be. Modern blues songs tend to be about hard times and personal or sexual relationships. Country blues often expressed the hard times of the African-American experience. But much more than today, early blues could also be comic, or present a casually humorous take on daily life.

Taking Measure of the 12-Bar Blues

Key Thought

The 12-bar blues is the most common blues form, but not the only one. Aside from big and small variations on the 12-bar blues itself, there are 8-bar blues and a variety of other forms based on folk, country, and ragtime songs.

Most blues songs take the form of the *12-bar blues,* so called because it consists of 12 bars (i.e., measures) of four beats each. There are three sung lines, each one fitting into a four-bar section. Almost always, the first line is sung twice, and then the thought is completed or answered by the final line.

A usual blues verse, with the chord changes in the key of E, looks like this:

Trouble last night and trouble the night before
Trouble last night and trouble the night before
Trouble in my home and trouble knocking at my door.

The words fit against a chord structure that you would strum out like this, with each slash representing one beat:

E	E	E	E	
////	////	////	////	

A	A	E	E	
////	////	////	////	

B7	A	E	E	E
//	//	////	////	////

Represented in music, the melody and strumming looks like this:

12-Bar Blues

188

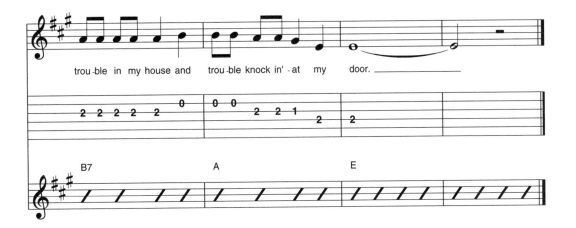

trou-ble in my house and   trou-ble knock in'-at   my   door. _____

Seventh Chords

We've just strummed through a blues using the E, A, and B7 chords. Perhaps you find that it doesn't sound all that bluesy yet. Play it again, but this time use a seventh chord every time, using these chord shapes.

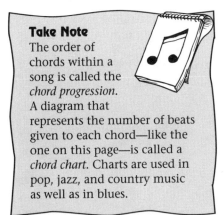

Take Note
The order of chords within a song is called the *chord progression*. A diagram that represents the number of beats given to each chord—like the one on this page—is called a *chord chart*. Charts are used in pop, jazz, and country music as well as in blues.

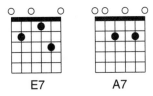

E7   A7

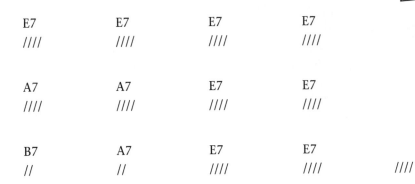

E7	E7	E7	E7	
////	////	////	////	
A7	A7	E7	E7	
////	////	////	////	
B7	A7	E7	E7	
//	//	////	////	////

189

Take Note
Blue notes are defined as the flatted third and seventh of the normal major scale.

Seventh chords sound bluesy because—depending on exactly which chords they are—they include some extra notes called *blue notes*.

Practice strumming these chord changes until you can play them smoothly before we go further. Keep the beat even, and try experimenting by choosing to play any given measure with either a plain chord or the seventh. If you don't know a plain B yet, just use B7. Once you get these chord changes automatic, you've got the blues.

Getting Down to the Blues

Key Thought
About half of all regular 12-bar blues have a chord progression exactly like this one. In the other, the second measure goes to A and but the third and fourth stay in E. This creates extra opportunity to vary the melody. Each time you learn a new 12-bar blues, you'll find it goes one way or the other.

Now let's build a blues solo. It will be based on a characteristic rhythm called a *shuffle* that also appears in rock, pop, country, and jazz. The shuffle beat has a loping feeling that comes from each foot-tap being divided evenly into thirds, or in musical language, *triplets*.

Tap your foot or clap your hands slowly and evenly. With each beat, say to yourself *one-two-three, one-two-three* as if you were saying *rock-a-bye, rock-a-bye*.

Now, instead of calling out three parts of the beat, let's work with two parts in a *LONG-short* rhythm. The *LONG* part takes up the first two-thirds of the beat, as if you were saying *BA-by*. You can go back and fourth between *one-two-three* and *LONG-short* in different combinations by reciting the syllables *"rock-a-bye, rock-a-bye, BA-by, BA-by," "rock-a-bye BA-by, rock-a-bye BA-by,"* and so on, in different combinations. Try reciting these syllables to yourself as you play the following example. To get a blues sound, sound all three notes by brushing upward with your index finger.

Guitar Gods

The deepest country blues came from the Mississippi Delta in the early part of the twentieth century, and the great master of *Delta blues* is Charlie Patten. However, his surviving records are so scratchy and primitively engineered that his followers like Son House, Tommy Johnson, and Robert Johnson are far more accessible. Texas, Arkansas, and Louisiana produced great stylists including Blind Lemon Jefferson, Lonnie Johnson, Lightnin' Hopkins, Big Bill Broonzy, and Robert Pete Williams. From the Virginia and Carolina flatlands come the so-called *Piedmont blues,* with a jaunty style more like the fingerpicking discussed in Chapter 19. Blind Blake, Elizabeth Cotten, Blind Boy Fuller, and Etta Baker are major exponents, and the wonderful style of Mississippi John Hurt also belongs here. Early white recording artists like Jimmie Rodgers, Frank Hutchison, and Maybelle Carter adapted African-American blues to their own tradition. Blues became electric and band oriented during the forties and fifties, and the playing of Muddy Waters, Otis Rush, Elmore James, Chuck Berry, and B. B. King is the bedrock of rock guitar. The sixties folk-music movement rediscovered the past masters of country blues and made new discoveries like Fred MacDowell and Mance Lipscomb. Today, powerful performers like Taj Mahal and Keb Mo' keep country blues alive by adding their contemporary personalities, and blues guitar techniques influence today's music pervasively.

Basic Shuffle

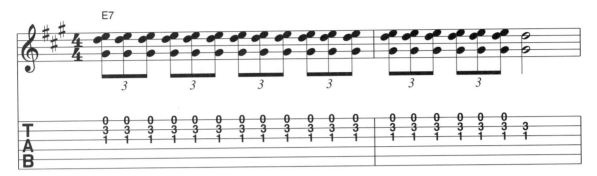

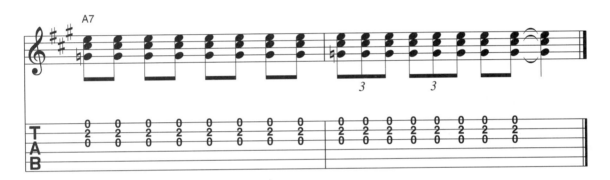

Now that we've got the basic beat, let's play the same music, adding a steady bass beat to reinforce the rhythm. Do this by playing a bass note steadily along with each foot tap, like so:

Shuffle with Bass

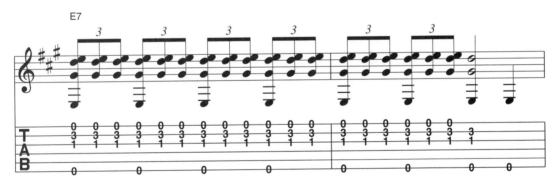

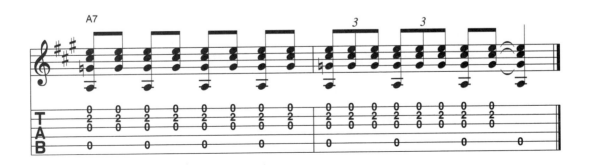

Key Thought

When you read a piece of music that has a shuffle beat, you should interpret two eighth notes with the *LONG-short* feeling rather than evenly. You'll know to do this when the music has an instruction like *swing, shuffle,* or *triplet feel* at the beginning.

Pick Hit

Playing a good shuffle is an art. It's not easy to get a feeling that's relaxed and exciting at the same time. Some performers like a lazy shuffle, while others can be intense. In either case, a good shuffle should make it impossible for you to stay still. Listen to John Lee Hooker and Canned Heat for some good shuffle beats.

Keeping that thumb absolutely steady should be your goal. Even the greatest guitarists sometimes miss a beat now and then, but they don't like it any more than you do.

Once the shuffle beat and the steady bass are under control, we can move on to some real blues playing. This piece has a classic country blues sound recalling the Delta and Texas styles. You'll be using these chord shapes. Learn them first and reading the piece will be easier.

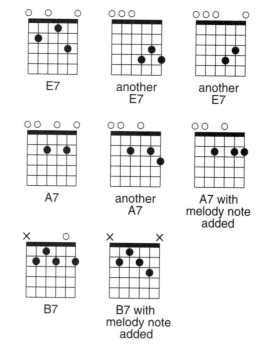

E7   another E7   another E7

A7   another A7   A7 with melody note added

B7   B7 with melody note added

Classic Country Blues

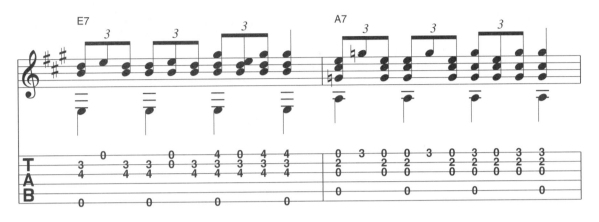

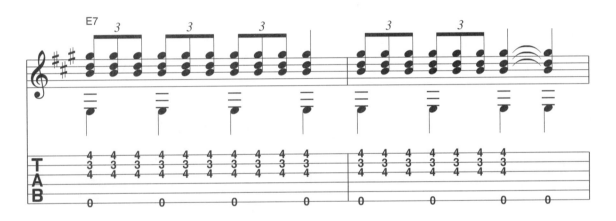

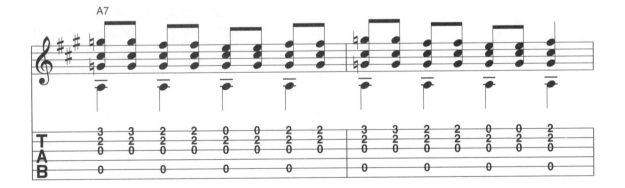

In Chapter 10, "Rythm Practice," you learned about syncopation. Here is an example of a 12-bar blues with what is called a "Walking Bass." Just as in Travis picking, you keep the thumb beats steady and lightly accent all the off-beats with the fingers.

Walkin Blues

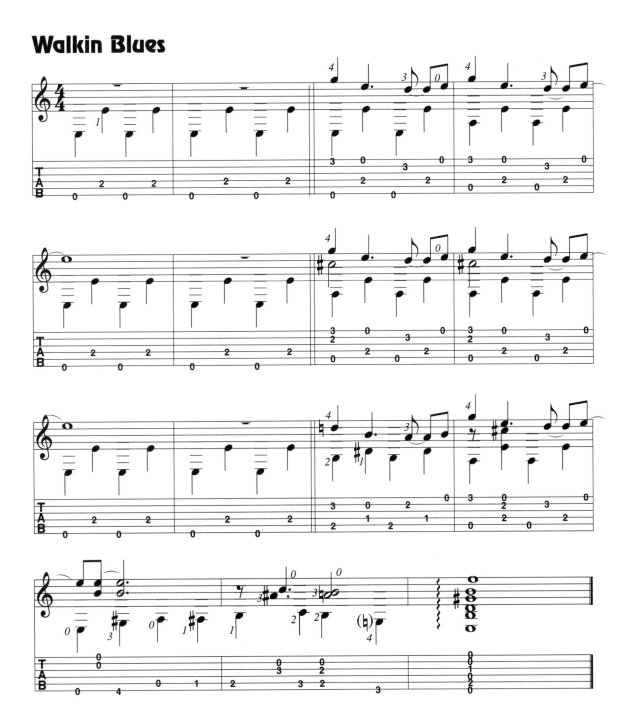

The Least You Need to Know

➤ There are various regional and chronological blues styles, but they all share similar song structures and the use of blue notes.

➤ Almost all 12-bar blues have the same chord structure with a few variations. This means that once you learn the 12-bar blues structure you have access to hundreds, even thousands, of songs.

➤ If you want a make a song sound bluesy, substitute seventh chords where plain chords are indicated.

195

Everybody dreams of playing rock guitar—the screaming fans! The flashing lights! The Spandex pants!

Today's rock is the mainstream American music, embracing so many genres that it's impossible to speak of a single guitar style. If *rock* means anything at all, it means a guitar-driven music as opposed to the piano- and wind-instrument-based pop of an earlier generation. Mention a *rock guitarist* and you'll probably visualize a heavy-metal maniac, full of screaming guitar licks and extravagant stage moves. But rock also produces anti-virtuosos who react against the musical show-offs by using deliberately simple guitar styles.

In view of the many ways rock guitar has branched out, it's fascinating to go back to its roots in fifties rock and rockabilly. Let's make rockabilly our introduction to rock guitar—with the extra advantage that it will sound good on acoustic as well as electric guitar. In this chapter, we'll learn a basic rockabilly/boogie accompaniment pattern, how to craft a rock-style solo, and then put it all together for a blazing rock workout!

Chapter 21

Rock and Roll

In this Chapter

➤ Basic rockabilly accompaniment

➤ The boogie bass

➤ Incorporating a rockabilly bass into a 12-bar blues song

➤ Crafting a Chuck Berry–style solo

➤ Putting it all together

Key Thought
Classic rockabilly guitar is based on the blues. If you haven't been through the blues chapter of this book, have a look at it now and get familiar with the chord structure of the 12-bar blues.

The Boogie Bass

An important sound in rock and rockabilly is the popular low-note figure called the *boogie-woogie* (or just *boogie*) bass, borrowed from the left-hand rhythms of blues pianists. We'll work in the key of A, using the chords A, D, and E to make up a blues.

Let's start with the boogie bass that goes with an A chord. On the fourth string, fret with your index and ring fingers and pluck the notes with a downstroke of either your thumb or a flatpick.

Guitar Gods

Rock guitar developed out of electric blues guitar and blues piano sounds. Chuck Berry was a giant influence. Among the early rock stars, players like Paul Burlison, Scotty Moore (with Elvis Presley), Les Paul, Eddie Cochran, Buddy Holly, Duane Eddy, James Burton (with Elvis Presley, Ricky Nelson, and Emmylou Harris), and Cliff Gallup (with Gene Vincent) all produced lasting sounds that have inspired others over the years. In the sixties, the Beatles' Paul McCartney and George Harrison ran with the ball and added many imaginative new elements, some of them inspired by the Indian sitar. Eric Clapton's extroverted work with Cream laid the foundations for heavy-metal guitar and the profusion of guitar gods who are today's rock Olympians.

Now let's add two things. First we'll double up the notes to give them a more insistent quality. Continue to pluck with downstrokes, keeping the beat even and steady. At the same time, let's pick with a slightly broader downstroke that catches the fifth string as well as the fourth, in order to get a fuller sound that suggests a chord.

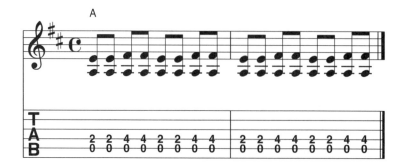

Once you've mastered this sound, it's not too hard to go on to the boogie-woogie figures that go with the D and E chords. Just make the identical moves, this time on the fourth and third strings for D and on the sixth and fifth strings for E, like so:

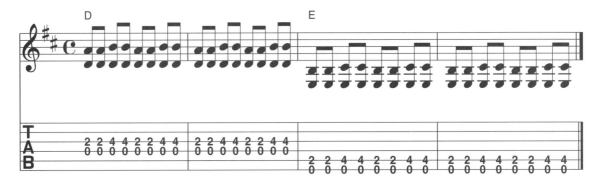

Now we'll just fit these bass figures that go with the A, D, and E chords into the structure of a 12-bar blues. A classic rockabilly guitar part is the result.

Classic Rockabilly

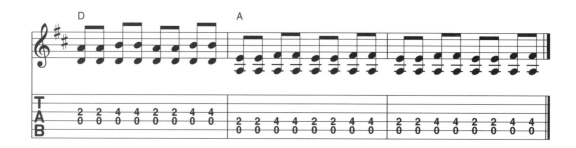

A High-Note Solo

Pick Hit
The original rockabillies like Elvis Presley, Gene Vincent, and Carl Perkins cultivated an image of informality and frantic craziness. Don't be deceived. They were professional show people who practiced as hard as anyone to put on a polished show—it wasn't one that fit the Broadway idea of polish that was prevalent at the time. So even though what you're playing is "only rock and roll," you will have to work to get it to sound good.

Now that we've got down a typical rhythm part, let's work on a high-note solo. We'll be using an sound that came into rockabilly mostly from the playing of Chuck Berry. Buddy Holly used it a lot. So did the Beatles, and rock and country guitarists continue to find new variations on it up to today.

First we need to review some of the basic theory that every guitarist must use to navigate the fingerboard—the chromatic scale. Notes are named by the musical alphabet that goes from A to G, and then starts over again. In between every letter, except B to C and E to F, lies another note that you can call by either of two names—sharp (meaning *higher than*) or flat (meaning *lower than*). Thus, the note that lies between A and B can be called either A-sharp or B-flat. Each note, including the sharps and flats, corresponds to one fret on the guitar.

For example, consider the A (fifth) string. The note of the open string is A, the note on the first fret is B-flat (or A-sharp), the second fret is B, the third fret is C, the fourth fret is D-flat, and so on. On the first or sixth strings, both E strings, the first fret would be F, the second fret F-sharp, and so on. Each box below represents one fret.

A	A-sharp/B-flat	B	C	C-sharp/D-flat	D
D-sharp/E-flat	E	F	F-sharp/G-flat		G
G-sharp/A-flat	A				

Let's apply this knowledge to chord shapes. Play a D chord. There it is, with its lowest notes on the second fret. Now move it up to the third fret. You just made it an E-flat (or D-sharp) chord. Move it up another fret and you'll be playing E. Play it on the fifth fret and it will become an F chord, and so on.

The same trick applies to every other chord shape. There's just one thing you have to be careful about. To keep extraneous notes out of the chord, be sure to sound only the strings that belong to the movable chord shape that you are fretting. Don't sound the open strings, because they are not being moved up along with the fingered strings. They won't necessarily give you the appropriate notes for the chord. (However, sometimes the open strings sound appropriate or even weirdly interesting along with a moved-up chord, anyway. You can experiment to find out.)

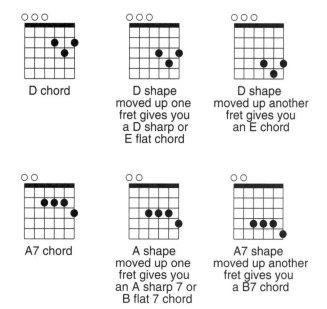

D chord

D shape
moved up one
fret gives you
a D sharp or
E flat chord

D shape
moved up another
fret gives you
an E chord

A7 chord

A shape
moved up one
fret gives you
an A sharp 7 or
B flat 7 chord

A7 shape
moved up another
fret gives you
a B7 chord

In this solo, we'll be using these basic chord shapes moved up the fingerboard:

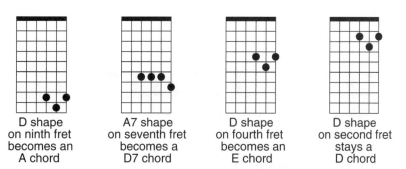

D shape
on ninth fret
becomes an
A chord

A7 shape
on seventh fret
becomes a
D7 chord

D shape
on fourth fret
becomes an
E chord

D shape
on second fret
stays a
D chord

Here goes our lead guitar solo. We'll be sounding only the highest three strings of the A7 chord, but if you've already learned this chord shape covering four strings, you may find it easier to keep fingering all four. With a flatpick, use energetic downstrokes. If you're playing finger style, brush down with your thumb, brush down with the nail of your index finger (and perhaps one or more other fingers as well), or brush up with your index finger across all three strings.

Key Thought
Rock music, like country and so many other popular styles, is based on rhythm. Don't get so carried away with lead guitar solo dreams that you never learn how to strum out a song with a steady beat. It's hard, probably impossible, to be a strong soloist if you can't play rhythm.

Lead Guitar Solo

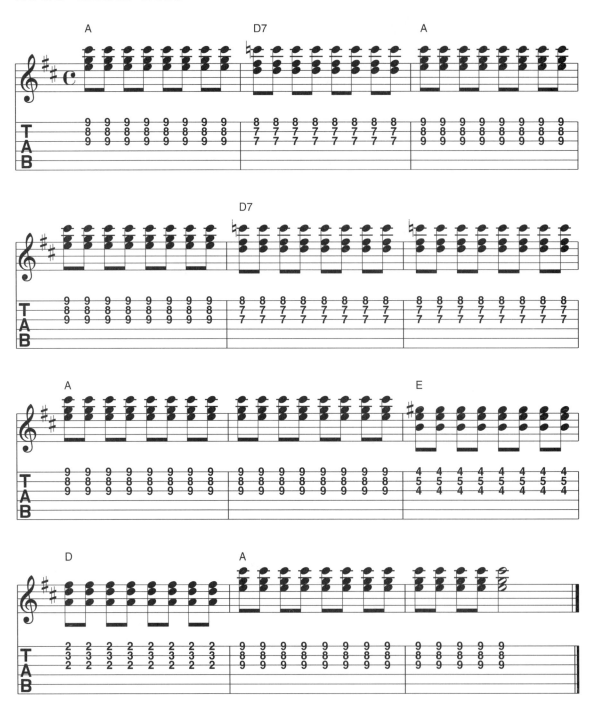

This lead will fit over the boogie-woogie bass we already learned. For the grand finale to this rock chapter, try teaching these parts to a friend and play them together, alternating with each other on bass and lead. To make it a little easier, here's how they look together:

Lead Guitar with Accompaniment

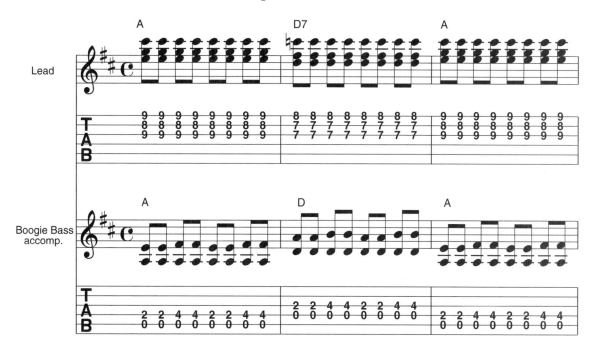

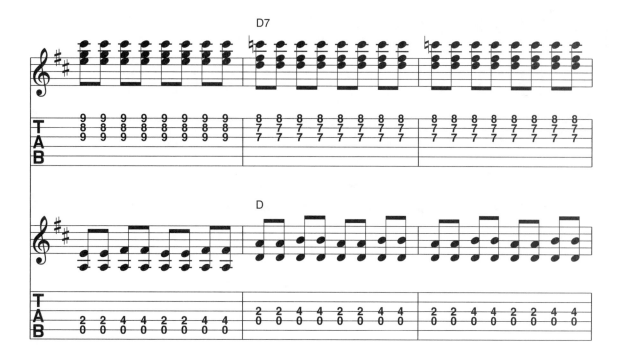

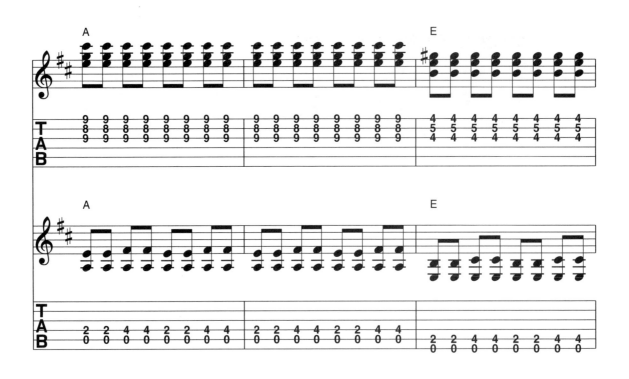

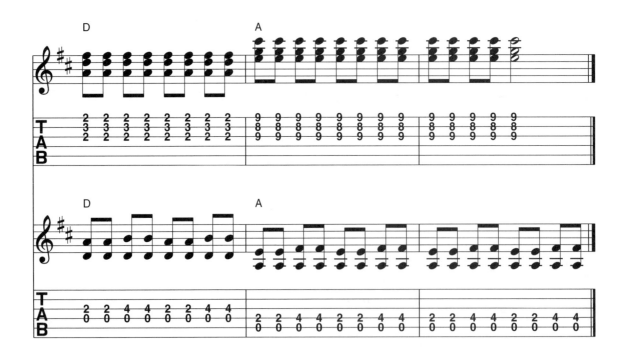

The Least You Need to Know

➤ Rockabilly and a great many other rock styles are based on the blues.

➤ Don't let casual stage appearances and crazy personal lives fool you. Playing in a rock band requires preparation and musical discipline.

➤ Most rock bands divide lead and rhythm functions between two guitarists.

➤ The chromatic scale is the single most valuable theoretical tool you need to find your way around the guitar. Some guitarists know little more, but it's hard to live without it.

Pick Hit
A famous heavy-metal guitarist admired for his pyrotechnic solos was once asked how he learned to play so fast. "By playing slowly," he answered. It's true. You can only play fast by working your speed up from perfection at a slow tempo.

Part 6
Taking Off

You're just about ready to leave the nest and take off on your own. But before you go there are a few more things I'd like to show you. Learning how to form chords will enable you to be a good all-around accompanist. Moving up the fingerboard will enable you to take full advantage of the guitar's range. Some secrets that guitar virtuosos have learned over the years will also be revealed. And finally, as my last gift to you, I have two beautiful showpieces for you to learn to impress your family and friends—and yourself!

Chord Formation

Most guitar players want to be able to play chords to accompany their singing or to play in a band. Learning different chords can give you a wider variety of accompanying techniques, and also can expand your capabilities.

In this chapter, we learn that certain chords bear special relationships to each other, and that these chords are likely to be used together in harmonizing a song. We see how the related chords can be derived from the major scale of any key, and how to build these in forms suitable to the guitar. We learn how to form the dominant, subdominant, and relative minor chords in any key, and also how to create some other useful chords that are in common use. Finally we use a chart known as a "chord clock" to aid transposition.

Take Note

Transposition means changing a piece from one key to another. For example, singing a song in the key of C might be out of your vocal range; by transposing it to G, you might be able to sing it comfortably.

Chord Families

It is very useful to understand the basics of chord construction and how chords relate to each other.

The most obvious case is the G7, which resolves naturally to the C chord, but in addition you will notice that many songs in the key of C use the F, Am, and Dm chords, all of which belong in the C chord family.

The best way to understand this is to look at the notes of the C-major scale.

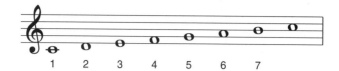

Major chords are made from the first, third, and fifth steps of the scale.

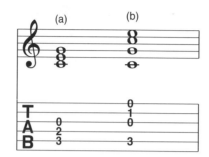

Here is the major chord built on the first note of the scale, known as the *tonic*. The three important notes are the C, E, and G. The second chord shown above is a familiar guitar version of the chord with more notes, but each of them is still a C, E, or G. When the notes are repeated, as in the case above where there are two Cs, the C is said to be *doubled*. In making bigger chords, the first and fifth may be freely doubled. Doubling the third doesn't sound as good. A chord can be made without the fifth, as in (a), below:

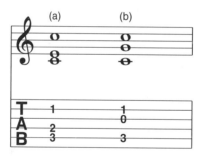

The chord still has some flavor of being a C chord. However, if you leave out the third, as in (b) above, the character is lost and the chord sounds hollow.

Related Chords

The most common related chords are those built on the fourth and fifth notes of the scale.

For simplicity, these chords are often referred to just by their number—usually with Roman numerals such as I, IV, and V. The V chord is G major in this case, and the G7 is formed by adding the seventh note above the G.

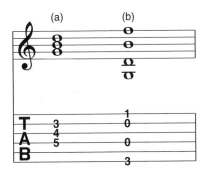

Here, (a) shows the necessary components of the G chord: G, B, and D.

The seventh note above G is F, and adding this as in (b) makes a familiar G7. The V chord is known as the *dominant*, and when the seventh is added it is known as the *dominant seventh*.

The IV chord, F in this case, is also known as the *subdominant*.

There are hundreds of songs that only use the I, IV, and V chords, and understanding this makes it easy to change key.

For instance, if you are in the key of C and the song feels too low for your voice, you can try D a tone higher. The V chord in D, counting up the scale, is A. A7 will be the dominant seventh. The fourth note of the D scale is G, so G will be the IV chord or subdominant. So everywhere you had C as I chord, you may substitute a D chord, and similarly you may replace the G7 chords with A7s, and the Fs with Gs.

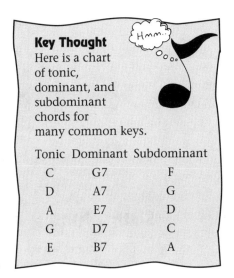

Key Thought
Here is a chart of tonic, dominant, and subdominant chords for many common keys.

Tonic	Dominant	Subdominant
C	G7	F
D	A7	G
A	E7	D
G	D7	C
E	B7	A

The Relative Minor

The other close relative is the chord built on the sixth note of the scale. Looking back to the C scale, you will see that this is the A, and that building up the three notes in the same way gives us an A-minor chord:

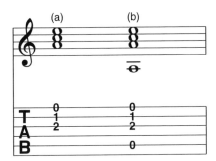

Here (a) shows the essential notes, and (b) a common guitar version with the A doubled.

Other Useful Chords

The Diminished Seventh

Diminished chords are easy to form: simply build up three minor thirds (one and a half tones) on top of any note to form its diminished seventh. There are really only three distinct diminshed chords, because all others share the same notes.

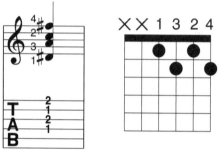

The upper staff shows the components of the C diminished seventh. Below is a useful movable diminished form. The D♯ diminished contains the same notes as the C.

Sixths, Ninths, and Major and Minor Sevenths

Other commonly used chords are the sixth, ninth, and major and minor seventh, formed as follows:

For the sixth, add the sixth note of the scale to the tonic (one) chord.

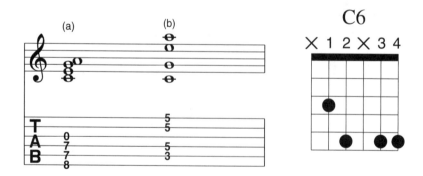

The ninth is formed by adding the ninth note to the dominant seventh.

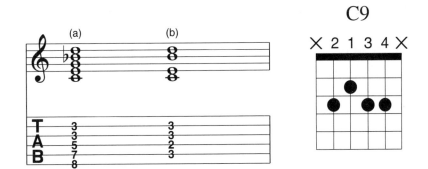

In this case, the C9 in root position is impractical on the guitar. Dropping the fifth (G) is acceptable, and results in a useful movable shape.

The minor seventh is formed by adding a seventh note to the minor chord.

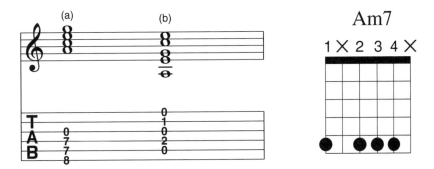

As before, the chord at (b) is more practical for the guitar, also the useful movable shape in the chord block.

The major seventh is formed by raising the seventh note of the dominant seventh by a half step:

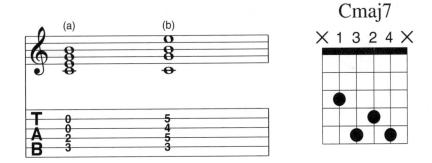

A glance at the sheet music of contemporary songs will show many chords altered from the common forms, particularly songs with a modern jazz flavor. Some sheet music gives chord blocks, but the quality of chords suggested is sometimes dubious. A better plan for enlarging your chord repertoire is to work through a classic book such as the one by George M. Smith, a former top Hollywood studio musician, which is still considered one of the best available.

Transposing with the Chord Clock

Finally, here is a chart that shows the common chords of each key. It also tells you how many sharps or flats belong to each key. Look to the right for the dominant, to the left for the subdominant, and below for the relative minor.

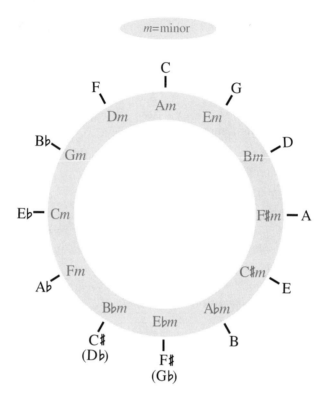

To take a very simple example, you might have a song in C major (no sharps or flats) and you want to put it up a tone to D. The song uses the chords of F and G. F and G are to the left and right of the C.

Move around to where you see the D. On each side may be found the equivalent chords, in this case G and A. That's all there is to it.

The Least You Need to Know

➤ Chords are used to accompany all types of music.

➤ There are three basic types of chords—the tonic, subdominant, and dominant—that are used to accompany hundreds of songs.

➤ Other common chords include the relative minor; sixth; ninth; and major, minor, and diminished sevenths.

➤ It's easy to transpose from key to key by knowing the relationships of these basic chords to the scale.

Chapter 23

Moving up the Fingerboard

In this Chapter

➤ The positions of the guitar

➤ How to change position

➤ The guide finger

➤ The portamento and slide

➤ Notes in the fifth position

➤ Study in E minor

➤ Easy Tárrega

➤ Plegaria

Traditionally easy guitar music has tended to be confined to the first four or five frets of the guitar. Usually beginners are reticent about learning and reading the notes in the higher positions.

However, remaining within that five-fret range imposes serious limitations on your playing and becomes boring after awhile. Learning the notes of the higher frets opens up a whole variety of more interesting music.

In this book, we have the advantage of tablature as a reminder of where the notes are at any part of the guitar, so we can proceed up the fingerboard to learn some interesting pieces that use more of the guitar.

The Positions of the Guitar

The positions of the guitar are numbered in similar fashion to other stringed instruments. In the first position, the left hand is in place to reach the first four frets on all strings. Similarly, in the fifth position the first finger would play at the fifth fret, and the notes of the fifth position would be frets five through eight on all strings.

So far we have mostly used notes in the first or second positions. Now it is time to learn some new notes and adventure further up the fingerboard.

Ways to Change Position

Straightforward chord playing often involves jumping from position to position, but more complex solos are usually fingered to take advantage of smoother ways to make the transitions. The simplest is when the move is covered by an open string, like this:

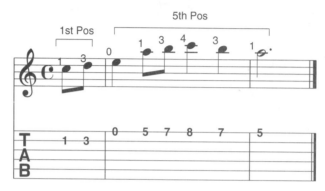

Using an open string

The open string rings over while the hand moves up.

The Guide Finger

Often the left hand finger can act as a guide up the string. This is one of the most common ways and it's important to understand.

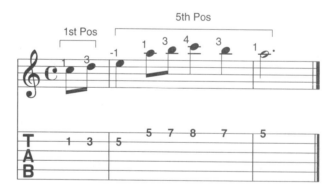

Here's the sequence. The first finger is used for the C, and stays on the string when the D is played. Then it travels up the string to the fifth fret without losing contact with the string. It doesn't have to press hard—just enough to keep contact and use the string as a guide rail. This movement is often shown with a small minus sign beside the destination finger (see the example above).

The Portamento

The *portamento* is a nice technique. It can make a position change easier, but it can also add a sound to the movement which, like a slur, adds smoothness to the musical passage. Here's an example:

The first note is played and held for almost its full time value. Then, with the note still sounding, the finger travels up the string to the fifth fret in time to play the E on the second beat. The small note indicates simply that the E is played normally to distinguish it from the slide (see below). The finger maintains a light pressure on the string, and there is a slight "scoop" sound as it moves up. This linking sound should not be too pronounced—the real secret is to leave the first finger in place until the last possible moment, and then to travel quickly up.

This is the kind of technique that requires experimentation until a satisfactory sound is achieved.

The Slide (Arrastre)

The slide, also known as the *arrastre,* is very similar to the portamento, except that the second note is *not* played by the right hand. The example below shows what happens.

➤ The C is played.

➤ The note is held for *almost* its full value. Just before the next beat, the finger slides up the string to arrive at the E exactly on the beat. The D will be heard, but obviously with diminished volume. Like the portamento, it has the effect of adding smoothness or *legato* to a passage.

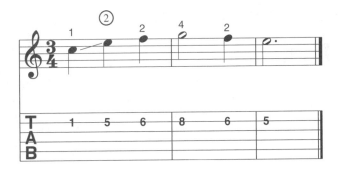

Notes of the Fifth Position

The chart shows the notes of the fifth position, and at once you will see some connections to help in remembering the notes.

Equivalent Notes

The guitar differs from keyboard instruments in that the same note can occur in different places. This is an advantage, because different tone colorations can be achieved by playing notes in different positions. Also, it also often facilitates keeping the hand in position without having to leap backward and forward to find the right notes.

Learning the equivalents is a device that some people use to memorize the higher position notes. For instance, you can see that the fifth fret of the second string is an E, and that it is the same note as the familiar open first string. Logically, the next note up will be the F, the same note as the F at the first fret on the first string. Continuing this research, you will find that every note in the fifth position is the same as one in the first position, with the exception of the higher notes A, B, and C on the first string.

You can even memorize notes when you're away from the guitar by simply working out where the equivalents have to be. Using logic to work this out helps fix the notes in the mind.

Here is an exercise to start familiarizing you with the fifth position. Try very hard to find the notes from the music notation before checking with the tablature below. The tablature is a crutch, and the sooner you can throw it away the better.

The circled number indicates the string in standard notation.

Natural Harmonics

Now we can tackle a really interesting piece, but first we need to learn one more technique—natural harmonics. This is quite easy once you get the feel of it.

When a string is touched lightly by a left-hand finger at exactly half its length and then plucked by the right hand, both halves can be made to vibrate, producing a bell-like sound. The secret is to take the left-hand finger away the instant the note has been played.

Notice in the first diagram that the finger is not on its tip but is parallel to the fingerboard. This makes it possible to touch several strings at once.

The second diagram shows the finger which has been quickly lifted away once the harmonic was played.

In position to play a harmonic

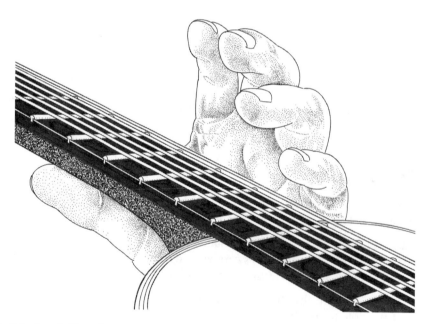

The finger is lifted quickly after the harmonic is played.

Try this out now, because you will need it for the piece below.

1. Place the finger lightly as shown, just touching the first string right above the twelfth fret.

2. Play the first string with a rest stroke about an inch away from the bridge. Playing closer to the bridge makes stronger harmonics.

3. Take the little finger off to allow the string to vibrate.

If you leave the finger on too long, the sound will be deadened. Next, try the same procedure but do it on the second and third strings. Finally, when you feel well synchronized, try for a chord on the top three strings. Obviously you cannot use a rest stroke with the right hand—just play the chord with *i, m,* and *a.*

The harmonic at the twelfth fret has the same pitch as a normal note played there. However, harmonics are often written with open strings, and a number for where to touch the string. The abbreviation *harm.* (for harmonic) or *arm.* (for *armonico*) is customarily used.

The harmonic at the twelfth fret is the strongest and easiest to play. Progressively weaker harmonics are found at the seventh, fifth, and fourth frets, with results as shown. These are shown doing the harmonics on the bottom string. The harmonic at the fourth fret is quite hard to sound clearly, and necessitates playing near the bridge with the right hand.

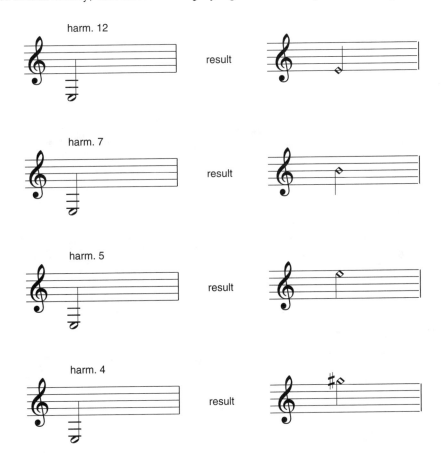

The study below, attributed to Francisco Tárrega, gives the opportunity to explore some higher notes and also to practice the harmonics. Try to use the notation, since this indicates fingering, bars, and so on.

The *a, m, i* arpeggio will be good practice for the Romance later on.

Study in E Minor (Francisco Tárrega)

Study Notes

This piece is easy to play once the *a, m, i* arpeggio has been practiced. Bring out the melody by giving slightly more emphasis to the first note of the three.

A. As explained in the text, these harmonics are done at the twelfth fret. You may wish to try it first with a single note. Then when you can achieve the harmonic sound try laying the little finger across the three strings as shown in the illustrations.

B. A four-string half bar is better than a three-string one here.

C. This is a big stretch. It is reasonable to let go of the bass G until you have practiced this enough to take the difficulty out of it.

Plegaria (Guillermo Gomez)

Study Notes

This charming and wistful piece gives you the opportunity to express your romantic feelings.

A. The third finger reaching across will feel strange at first. However, this fingering makes it much easier to find the chord after the D♯.

B. Play the harmonics at the twelfth fret exactly as described in the text and illustrations.

C. Notice that the C is natural here.

D. After playing each half twice according to the repeat signs, go back to the beginning of the piece (D.C.) and play through to the point marked FINE.

The Least You Need to Know

➤ The left hand can comfortably cover about four or five frets in range.

➤ Moving the left hand up the neck is said to change it to a higher position. The fifth position, for example, is defined as locating the left hand to reach frets five to eight.

➤ Changing positions helps us play higher notes on the guitar more easily.

➤ A portamento is a glide between two notes, in which each note is played by the right hand. A slide is a similar motion, except the second note is not played but simply sounds as the fretting finger arrives.

➤ Sometimes it's easier to play a note on a different string to facilitate fingering.

➤ By lightly damping a string, we can produce bell-like tones called harmonics. This is an important effect in many pieces.

Chapter 24

Classical Virtuoso Secrets

In this Chapter

➤ The magic trick

➤ Tone production

➤ Vibrato

➤ The tremolo

➤ Developing good practice habits

➤ The importance of listening

This chapter is for those who feel they may want to pursue a serious interest in the classical style. There is a deep-seated belief, which I shared at one time, that there was a special "trick" that could be learned by studying with the right person. However, after participating in master classes of both Andrés Segovia and Julian Bream, I realized that there was no magic trick that would achieve instant results and take the place of hard work. However, there *were* some clear guidelines to making the best of one's potential—some related to technique, some to study habits, and some to activities away from the guitar. Here are some of my conclusions.

Tone Production

You've probably had the experience of hearing a great guitarist with a distinctive tone and wondering how it is achieved. You can buy the same instrument, play under the same conditions, and still come nowhere near equalling the sound that she or he achieves.

The magic of the classical guitar rests very much in the tone quality produced by the player, and as with the violin there can be distinctive differences in the tone produced by leading players. It is often surprising to find how much this individual quality can survive changes of instrument, and how a really good player can extract an amazing quality from a humble violin or guitar.

Frederick Noad learns the trick.

At the heart of quality tone production is the way the rest and free strokes are performed, as introduced in Chapter 7. With the rest stroke some of the factors involved are these:

1. Is the string made to vibrate vertically or horizontally in relation to the soundboard? It makes a distinct difference, and usually the more vertical vibration is preferable.

2. Where is the note played in relation to the bridge or sound hole? Closer to the bridge, the sound will be more metallic. In contrast, the roundest sound will be achieved if the string is played at a point halfway between the left-hand fretting finger and the bridge. Try this out to hear the difference:

First, play the note near the bridge and pull the finger across in a free stroke that just clears the second string, vibrating the string in a plane parallel to the top of the guitar.

Now, with the same note prepared, play a rest stroke over the sixteenth fret, pressing the string down so that the vibration is as vertical as possible. Notice the considerable difference. For an even sweeter sound, play the same A at the tenth fret of the second string. Play your rest stroke at a point halfway between the tenth fret and the bridge, and press the string down for the roundest sound.

Guitar Gods

Ida Presti, an outstanding classical performer and interpreter, was born in Suresnes, France on May 31, 1924. She gave her first public recital at the age of 8, and later toured extensively in France and abroad. She had great technical facility and sometimes played with dazzling speed—Andrés Segovia once affectionately called her "Ida Prestissimo." In addition, her interpretations were profound and distinctive.

In 1952 Presti met guitarist Alexandre Lagoya, and a year later they were married. Thus was formed a guitar duo considered one of the finest ever. Together they performed some two thousand concerts around the world and made some outstanding recordings on the Philips label. Presti's premature death in 1967 was a great loss to the world. After a five-year break, Lagoya returned to an active concert career both as a soloist and with other distinguished musicians.

Vibrato

With the whole family of stringed instruments the *vibrato* technique can be used to make variations in the tone. The variation is actually one of pitch, caused by moving the left hand finger backward and forwards in line with the string. The fingertip does not lose contact, nor does the thumb. The hand is simply made to oscillate sideways along the same plane as the strings.

Try this:

Put the second finger on the E at the fifth fret of the second string. Play a rest stroke over the sound hole, and try oscillating the hand as described above. Remember to keep both thumb and finger in contact. Try the note with and without vibrato and notice the difference. Then experiment with notes all over the guitar. You will find the vibrato most effective above the fourth fret.

Below the fourth fret, the sideways vibrato is sometimes used, where the string is pushed back and forth on the fingerboard at right angles to the plane of the strings. This has to be done with subtlety so as not to sound like a blues bend, and is in fact rarely used.

The vibrato is rarely notated, the abbreviation "vib." being the most used indication.

The sounds that most tend to amaze the listener are those produced by a really well-executed scale, arpeggio or tremolo passage.

Tremolo

Because the guitar is not capable of a long sustained melody note, a *tremolo* is sometimes employed to repeat notes fast enought to give the impression of a continuous line.

In classical playing, tremolo usually consists of a bass note followed by three melody notes:

Tremolo

The most famous tremolo study is that of Francisco Tárrega, entitled "Recuerdos de la Alhambra," and thousands have been inspired to take up the guitar by Segovia's beautiful playing of this piece. Thousands have also tried unsuccessfully to master it.

A similar pattern is used in flamenco, except that there are four melody notes instead of three:

The flamenco tremolo

To play either form of tremolo evenly and up to time takes much practice.

Dividing your Practice Time

Becoming a good musician obviously involves an investment of time. Professional musicians are known to practice many hours, though this is usually broken up into segments. Segovia used to practice in sessions of one and a quarter hours with a break in between. Usually this would involve two sessions in the morning and a third in the afternoon. Sometimes there was even a fourth, depending on circumstances such as travel, performances, etc. A few very fortunate virtuosi are able to maintain a high performance level with less practice. This usually relates to extraordinary natural aptitude and a start in early childhood.

Most people do not have unlimited practice time, so it becomes important to divide up what is available into the most productive segments. A smaller amount of practice on a daily basis achieves more than a periodic onslaught. The latter can produce overstrained muscles and tendons and becomes counterproductive after an hour or two. Daily practice develops the muscles evenly and maintains them in peak form.

Practice time needs to be divided so as to cover certain main topics. These include:

1. Purely technical practice for muscular development and maintenance.
2. Work on the current new piece.
3. Some sight-reading of new material.
4. Performance of existing repertoire.

The first phase is important for the improvement and maintenance of mechanical skills. It is rewarding in the sense that results are seen fairly quickly. However, technique should not become the only goal because it is the means, not the end. This phase is best done first, because it serves to warm up the fingers.

Phase two involves the process of learning a new piece, from initial reading to final memorization and polishing. It is good to do this early in the practice period when the mind is fresh and able to cope with the necessary detailed concentration.

Phase three is probably the one most neglected by amateurs. However, the results of reading even one line of unknown music a day are phenomenal. A surprisingly good level of reading can be achieved in a year, particularly if a separate effort is made to learn the keyboard really well.

The final phase is probably the most enjoyable and should not be neglected. It involves the playing of repertoire that has already been learned and memorized, mainly for pleasure but with the advantage of some polishing of the final version. This also keeps a number of pieces available for performance, should the occasion arise. A good player will want to perform, whether for friends and family, at a guitar society, or at some more formal venue.

Additional Study

Probably the most important part of becoming a musician is listening to a wide variety of music, ancient and modern, solo and orchestral, classical and popular. By listening you develop your taste as well as your knowledge. At the top of the list is always live performance. As good as modern recordings are, they can never quite substitute for an actual event. However, recordings and the radio will of necessity provide the main source.

The Least You Need to Know

➤ There is no magic trick.
➤ Tone quality is the key to "virtuoso" sound.
➤ Good practice habits speed up progress.
➤ Listening to all varieties of music is important.

Putting It All Together

After a number of years of experience in this field, I have found that certain pieces have a magic quality to them that draws people to the guitar. Some are difficult, such as the tremolo study mentioned above, or the *Asturias* of Albéniz that is the goal of many players; but some are more approachable, providing they are systematically studied and practiced, and still have a magic quality when they are played well.

Some years ago I was in Alicante, in Southern Spain, enjoying an excellent flamenco performance in an old castle. During a break, the guitarist came over to meet our group and I was introduced as a classical player. Immediately he asked if I could show him a certain piece that he was obsessed with learning. He was a wonderful player, but didn't read music at all. He played his impression of the first measure, and I recognized a study by Fernando Sor. The session went on until about 4 A.M., and at every break the guitarist came over to learn and memorize another few measures.

The purpose of telling this story is twofold—first, that it is terribly frustrating to be a good guitarist with no reading skills, and second, that Sor's Study in B Minor, op. 35, no. 22, is a knockout piece worth studying at any level.

Study in B Minor (Fernando Sor)

Study Note, Study in B Minor

There is much barring in this piece, but fortunately the bars are alternated with unbarred passages that give the hand a chance to relax. Be sure to check your bar position, and although only five strings are involved in many of the chords, bar all six—the position is more reliable.

The particular beauty of this piece can be brought out by giving special attention to the melody notes—those marked with upward stems. Rest strokes may be used to give a fuller sound, and very occasionally vibrato may be used, for instance on the D that begins the last measure of the third line. This is a moment when the hand is released from holding a full chord so a moment may be snatched to make a really good sound.

A. The second finger is used here because it is very difficult to move the first finger from playing a note on the the first string right across the guitar to make a bar for the next note.

Advanced players use what they call a *hinge* bar. The E♯ would be played by the first finger but right at its base as if in bar position. The rest of the finger would be raised at an angle to enable the open B to sound. Then the finger slides forward to the second fret and drops to form the bar. This is tricky, but used extensively by the pros.

B. Be sure to place a *full* bar here in preparation for the next measure. It is awkward to jump from a half bar to a full bar.

C. The first finger has a long jump from the C down to the E♯ in the next measure. The secret is to take the chord off just before the end of the measure—the open G ringing on covers the gap.

D. This line needs special practice. First, it is an awkward move for the first finger to go from the top string to barring the fourth fret. However, there is no reasonable alternative, so just repeat the movement a few times, and try to ease gracefully into the bar rather than grabbing at it.

E. A touch of vibrato on the B is attractive here, and even a small hesitation marking the end of the upward climb.

F. The half bar here rather breaks the rule of trying to avoid going from half to full bars on the same fret. However, there are no reasonable alternatives, since most players would find a full bar here uncomfortable.

Romance Anónimo (Anonymous Romance)

The Anonymous Romance that follows also has stories attached to it, although no one can say authoritatively where it comes from. It is assumed to be Spanish because it was widely played there under the name *Romance Anónimo,* but some Spaniards believed it came from the Caucasus region. It was used in the film *Blood and Sand,* played by Vicente Gomez, and later in the French film *Jeux Interdits* (Forbidden Games), in which the performer was Narcisso Yepes. The piece was immediately popular, and in Europe is still referred to as "Jeux Interdits."

The Romance is harder to play than the Sor's Study in B Minor because of some stretches and extensive barring in the second section. However, there will be some who will go to almost any lengths to play the piece, so here it is.

Romance Anónimo

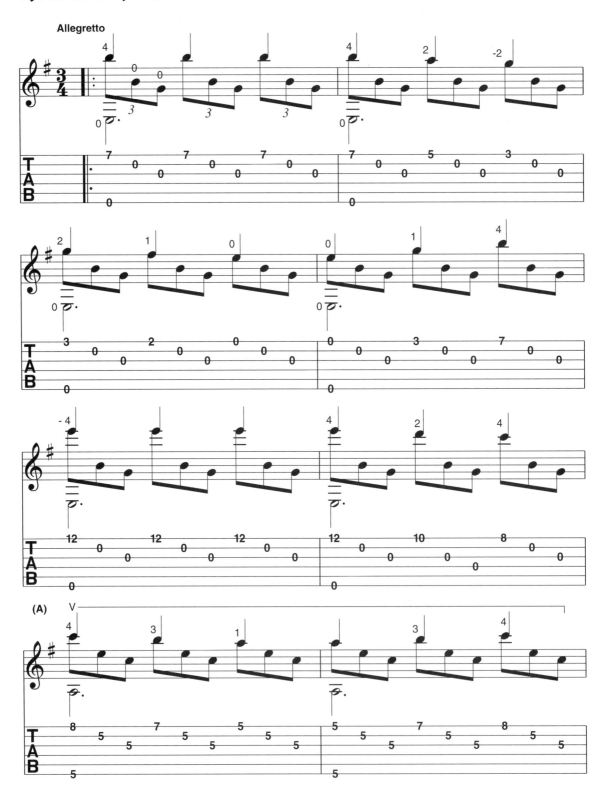

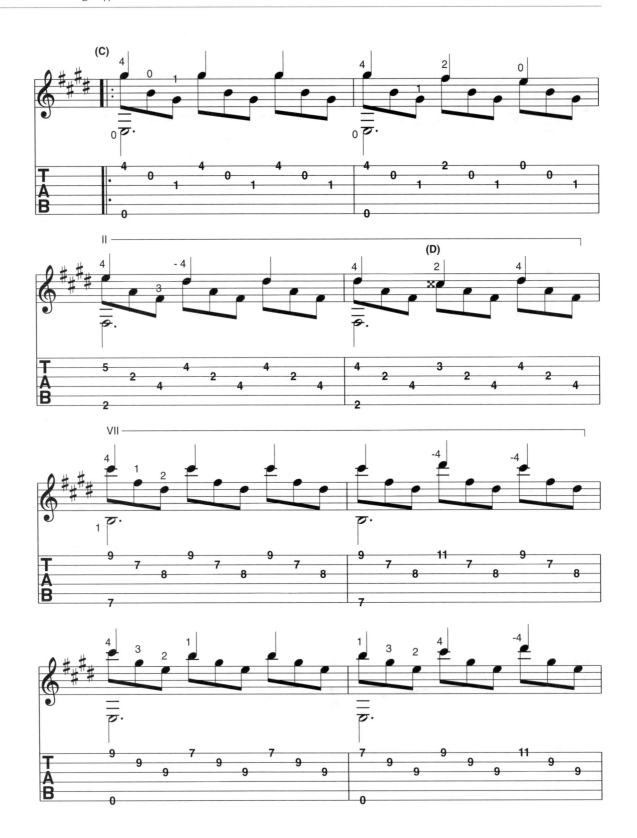

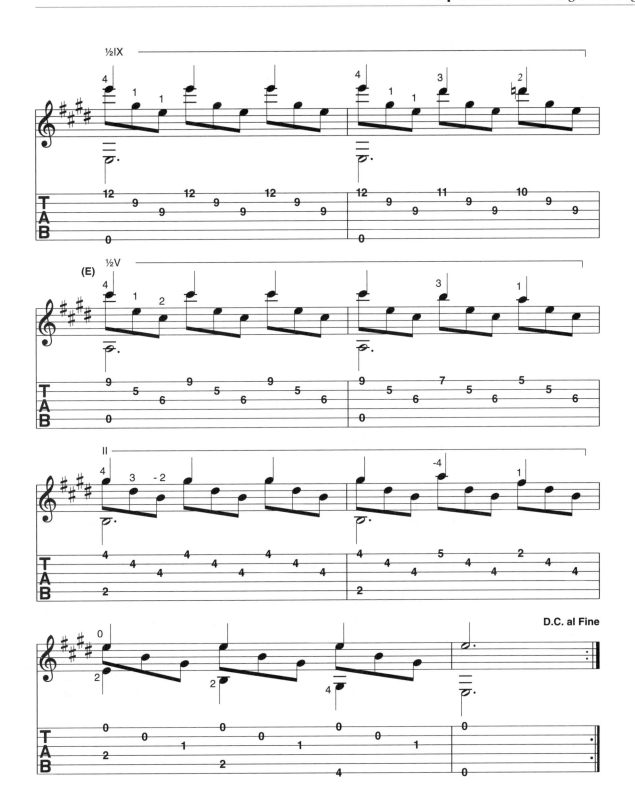

Study Notes, Romance Anónimo

The arpeggio form is the same as that of the Tárrega study in Chapter 23. If you have not already worked on that piece I would suggest doing so now, since it works as an excellent preparatory study.

Played as a straight arpeggio, i.e., free-stroke throughout, it sounds fine provided that an effort is made to bring out the melody. This can be done by playing the second and third notes of each triplet group slightly softer than the first. However, an occasional rest stroke on the first note of the measure can really make the melody sing. Even if this is done only every two measures, it still gives a more dynamic quality than a plain arpeggio. It is worth practicing the arpeggio by itself until the rest stroke with the ring finger feels natural.

A. Although you could get by with a half bar here the full bar is really better. The reason is that in a moment you have to move to a full bar at the seventh fret, and it is much more awkward to change from a half to a full bar rather than simply sliding a full bar up two frets. Try it both ways and you'll be convinced.

B. Obviously this is a practice spot, since the stretch to the eleventh fret is hard. The secret is a really good bar position to start with. After this measure it is plain sailing to the end of the section.

C. The second half is harder than the first due to the sustained bars and some large stretches. However, what seems impossible at first becomes feasible with repetition.

D. The sign × is for a double sharp, which raises the original note by *two* half steps. It is sometimes noted with two sharp signs side by side (♯♯). The same notes could have been written by writing three Ds, with the middle one having a natural sign (♮). However, three Ds in a row would disguise the musical line.

A double sharp is cancelled by a natural sign, with a sharp to the right of the natural if the note is to revert from double sharp to single sharp (the usual case). This could have been written by the C that begins the next measure, but is not strictly necessary because of the barline.

The move to the seventh position bar is a tough one, but there is no solution except extra practice.

E. Usually a four-string half bar is better than a three-string one; however, in this case covering three strings is as much as most people can manage. The second finger can be used to guide the hand down to the second-position bar in the last line.

Overall this is an easy piece for the right hand once the arpeggio pattern becomes familiar. However, the left-hand stretches require a certain opening up of the hand which comes with regular playing and practice. Never push the left hand too hard. If it begins to feel strained, stop playing and lay the hand flat on a table with the fingers slightly apart.

The Least You Need to Know

➤ There are some pieces that almost all classical guitarists enjoy playing.

➤ These pieces are hard to master but can become a central part of your repertory.

Further Study

Works by Frederick Noad

Frederick Noad has written a number of works directed to further development in different areas, as follows:

First Book for the Guitar (3 parts, or available together in an omnibus edition)
G. Schirmer Inc., New York

As the title implies, this book was written for the complete beginner. The earlier instruction and repertoire selections are mostly in the first and second positions, which makes this the easiest book for young beginners. The "how-to" sections are fully illustrated with line drawings.

Solo Guitar Playing (2 vols.)
Schirmer Books, a division of Macmillan Publishing Co., Inc., New York

This is a graded course in classical guitar performance that is widely used in colleges and music schools. The higher positions are introduced in a logical progression, and there is a large collection of repertoire pieces. Two audio cassettes and a CD are available as a supplement to vol. 1, which comprise recordings of all the exercises and repertoire contained in the book.

Vol. 2 deals in detail with the style of different periods of music, and leads to more advanced technique and musicianship.

100 Graded Classical Studies
Music Sales, Inc., New York

This book contains a selection from the best didactic studies of Fernando Sor, Mauro Giuliani, Matteo Carcassi, and Ferdinando Carulli. The studies are graded in order of difficulty, presenting a logical path for the gradual and progressive improvement of technical ability.

Dating from the earliest period of popularity of the classical guitar these famous études are a must for the serious student. The complete *25 Melodious Studies of Matteo Carcassi* are included.

Playing the Guitar
Schirmer Books, a division of Macmillan Publishing Co., Inc., New York

Frederick Noad's first book, now in its third edition, covers a wide range of guitar styles including folk songs, blues, fingerpicking, and flamenco. In addition to explaining tablature and music notation the book contains easy classical repertoire as well as fully written-out examples of the different playing styles.

The Renaissance Guitar
Ariel Music Publications, a division of Music Sales, Inc., New York

The Renaissance Guitar is the first in a series of historical collections of guitar music, with a selection from the best solos, duets, and songs from each period. The anthologies are profusely illustrated and contain biographical information about the composers and information on the musical styles of each period. These well-known collections are in the library of almost all serious classical guitarists. Audio cassette recordings have recently been added to assist students in finding and preparing pieces they really like.

Other books in this series are *The Baroque Guitar, The Classical Guitar,* and *The Romantic Guitar.*

The Guitar with Frederick Noad (video)
D & H Sales, North Hollywood, Calif.

24 video lessons in the Spanish/classical style, as broadcast on educational television.

Books

It is impossible to review the many books and videos (let alone list them all), but here is a fairly comprehensive list of recommended works. Most of these should be available in your local music store or by mail order. "Includes CD/cassette" means that an audio supplement is included. "CD/cassette available" means that you can purchase these items separately. Some of the books are quite specialized, so check that they reflect the area of your interest before buying.

General Instruction

The Complete Guitarist by Richard Chapman

The Guitar Handbook by Ralph Denyer

The Acoustic Guitar Guide by Larry Sandberg

Abe and Malka's 100 Guitar Accompaniment Patterns

Alfred's Basic Guitar Method: Book 1

Mel Bay's Modern Guitar Method 1 by Mel Bay. Cassette available

Mel Bay's Modern Guitar Method 2 by Mel Bay

Mel Bay's Modern Guitar Method 3 by Mel Bay

Arlen Roth's Complete Acoustic Guitar by Arlen Roth

Hal Leonard Guitar Method Book 1 by Will Schmid. Includes CD

The Complete Guitar Player Omnibus Edition by Russ Shipton

Dictionary of Strum and Picking Patterns by Fred Sokolow. Includes cassette or CD

Fretboard Roadmaps—The Essential Guitar Patterns That All the Pros Know and Use by Fred Sokolow

Teach Yourself Guitar by Harry Taussig

Basic Guitar Lessons, Book 1 by Happy Traum

Acoustic Guitar Basics by Keith Wyatt. Includes CD

Electric Guitar Basics by Keith Wyatt. Includes CD

Chords and Theory

Deluxe Encyclopedia of Guitar Chords by Bill Bay

Mel Bay's Deluxe Guitar Scale Book by Mel Bay

Guitar Scales in Tablature by William Bay

The Advanced Guitar Case Chord Book by Askold Buk

Uncle Tim's Building Blocks: A Visual Way to Learn Guitar Passages by Tim Gillespie

Uncle Tim's Book of Chords: A Visual Way to Construct Chords on the Guitar by Tim Gillespie

Transpositional Dial by Ron Green

Guitar Chord Encyclopedia by Steven Hall and Ron Manus

Contemporary Chord Khancepts by Steve Khan

Practical Theory for Guitar by Don Latarski. Includes CD

The Guitarist's Picture Chord Encyclopedia by John Pearse

Scales over Chords—How to Improvise and Never Play a Wrong Note by Wilbur M. Savidge and Randy Lee Vradenburg

Incredible Chord Finder by Will Schmid

Understanding Chord Progressions for Guitar

Complete Scales for All Guitarists (with Note Finder Poster) by Harvey Vinson

Guitar Fitness—An Exercising Handbook by Josquin des Pres

Flamenco

Mel Bay's Juan Serrano: Flamenco Concert Selections

Mel Bay's Juan Serrano: Flamenco Guitar, Basic Techniques by Juan Serrano. Includes CD

The Keys to the Flamenco Guitar by Dennis Koster. Includes cassette

Advanced Flamenco Guitar by Dennis Koster. Includes cassette

Rock and Blues

Beginning Fingerstyle Blues Guitar by Arnie Berle and Mark Galbo

How to Play Reggae Guitar by Ray Hitchins. Includes CD

Experience Hendrix—Beginning Guitar Method by Michael Johnson. Includes CD

The Anthology of Blues Guitar by Woody Mann

Teach Yourself Rhythm Guitar by Mark Michaels

Fundamentals of Funk for Guitar by Ronald Muldrow

Best of Blues Guitar by Fred Sokolow. Includes CD

Funk Rock by Troy Stetina. Includes CD

Acoustic Blues Guitar by Kenny Sultan. Includes CD

Blues Guitar Legends by Kenny Sultan. Includes CD

Country, Folk, and Fingerpicking

The Art of Contemporary Travis Picking by Mark Hanson

The Art of Solo Fingerpicking: How to Play Alternating-Bass Fingerstyle Guitar Solos by Mark Hanson

The Folk Music Source Book by Larry Sandberg and Dick Weissman

Jazz

Mickey Baker's Complete Course in Jazz Guitar, Book 1

Jazz Guitar Handbook by Alan de Mause. Includes CD

Fingerstyle Jazz Guitar: Teaching Your Guitar to Walk by Paul Musso. Includes CD

Al Di Meola taught by Al Di Meola

Pat Martino—Creative Force Part 1

Pat Martino—Creative Force Part 2

Bebop and Swing Guitar with Emily Remler

Videos

Basic/Introductory Videos

Beginning Guitar with Tom Chapin taught by Tom Chapin

Guitar Basics taught by Mike Christiansen

Beginning Electric Guitar taught by Arlen Roth

You Can Play Guitar, Vol. 1 taught by Happy Traum

Guitar Basics, Step One—For Electric or Acoustic taught by Keith Wyatt

Guitar Basics, Step Two—For Acoustic Guitar taught by Keith Wyatt

Guitar Basics, Step Two—For Electric Guitar taught by Keith Wyatt

Rock

Beginner's Rock Guitar taught by Fred Sokolow

Rockabilly Guitar taught by Fred Sokolow

Classical and Flamenco

Brazilian Music for Acoustic Guitar by Carlos Barbosa-Lima

Juan Martin: Learn Flamenco Guitar, Vol. 1

Blues

Robert Johnson Starlicks Master Session taught by Scott Ainslie

Blues by the Book—Fingerstyle Guitar taught by Roy Bookbinder

Advanced Fingerpicking Guitar Techniques: Blues Guitar taught by Stefan Grossman

Beginner's Blues Guitar taught by Fred Sokolow

Acoustic Blues Guitar taught by Kenny Sultan

Blues Guitar Legends: In the Styles of Lightnin' Hopkins and Blind Blake taught by Kenny Sultan

Fingerstyle

Celtic Airs, Jigs, Reels, and Hornpipes taught by Duck Baker

Flatpicking

Flatpicking the Gospels by Steve Kaufman

Easy Gospel Guitar taught by Steve Kaufman

An Intimate Lesson with Tony Rice

Doc Watson: Fingerpicking and Flatpicking

Flatpicking with Doc taught by Doc Watson, with Steve Kaufman

Guitar Gods

Here's a list of some of the guitarists you will want to know.

Laurindo Almeida (1917–1996)   Brazilian guitarist who helped popularize the bossa nova in the United States.

Chet Atkins (b. Chester Burton Atkins, 1924)   Country guitarist and record producer.

Jeff Beck (1944)   British-born blues/rock guitarist famous for his work with the Yardbirds and various other groups.

Chuck Berry (1926)   American pioneering rock guitarist, vocalist, and songwriter.

Blind Blake (c. 1895–c. 1930)   Chicago-based blues guitarist and vocalist known for his ragtime-influenced style of fingerpicking.

Mike Bloomfield (1944–1981)   Chicago-born blues/rock guitarist.

Julian Bream (1933)   English classical guitarist.

Lindsey Buckingham (1947)   Guitarist famed for his work with the group Fleetwood Mac.

Matteo Carcassi (1792–1853)   Italian guitarist who is the author of *25 Melodious Studies* still played today.

Ferdinando Carulli (1770–1841)   Italian guitarist who composed a famous guitar method that is still in use.

Charlie Christian (1916–1942)   American jazz guitarist who pioneered the use of the electric guitar and playing single-note melody lines.

Eric Clapton (b. Eric Patrick Clapp, 1945)   Virtuoso English blues guitarist.

Ry Cooder (1947)   Eclectic American fingerstyle guitarist and composer.

Francesco Corbetta (c. 1615–1681)   Italian guitarist who published many fingerstyle compositions.

Steve Cropper (1941)   Memphis guitarist famous for his work with Booker T and the MGs and session work for Stax Records.

Robert de Visée (c. 1660–c. 1720)   French guitarist who played for Louis XIV.

Bo Diddley (b. Elias McDaniel, 1928)   Mississippi-born rock guitarist and vocalist famous for the "Bo Diddley" beat.

Bob Dylan (b. Robert Zimmerman, 1941)   American singer/songwriter and guitarist.

Duane Eddy (1938)   American electric guitarist known for his "twangy" instrumental style.

Melissa Etheridge (1961)   Kansas-born rock guitarist and vocalist.

David "The Edge" Evans (1961)   Lead guitarist for the Irish rock group U2.

Leo Fender.   American electric guitar builder, famous for designing the Fender Telecaster and Stratocaster.

Jerry Garcia (1942–1995)   California-born rock guitarist and leader of the Grateful Dead.

Orville Gibson   American mandolin and guitar maker who was among the first to make carved-top instruments.

Mario Giuliani (1781–1829)   Italian guitarist who settled in Northern Europe.

Jimi Hendrix (b. James Marshall Hendrix, 1942–1971)   American rock guitarist known for his flamboyant stage presence and amazing technique.

Buddy Holly (b. Charles Edward Holley, 1936–1959)   American rock-and-roll guitarist who helped popularize the Fender Stratocaster.

Joan Jett (b. Joan Larkin, 1960)   American rock guitarist/vocalist.

Robert Johnson (c. 1900–c. 1939)   Mississippi blues guitarist famous for his intense playing style.

B. B. King (b. Riley B. King, 1925)   American blues guitarist who plays a Gibson electric guitar he named "Lucille."

Barney Kessell (1923)   American jazz guitarist known for his sweet style.

Mark Knopfler (1949)   Scottish-born rock guitarist and leader of the group Dire Straits.

Eddie Lang (b. Salvatore Massaro, 1902–1933)   Pioneering American jazz guitarist.

Leo Kottke   American acoustic guitarist.

Leadbelly (b. Huddie Ledbetter, 1889–1949)   American 12-string guitarist and songwriter who played blues and popular songs.

Christian Friedrich (C. F.) Martin   Legendary guitar maker born in Vienna who settled in Nazareth, Pennsylvania, and developed the modern X-braced guitar.

John McLaughlin (1942)   British-born, fleet-fingered jazz/rock guitarist.

Memphis Minnie (b. Lizzie Douglas, 1897–1973)   American blues guitarist famous for her popular recordings with husband Kansas City Joe (McCoy).

Wes Montgomery (b. John Leslie Montgomery, 1923–1968)   American popular jazz guitarist.

Ramón Montoya (1880–1949)   Spanish flamenco guitarist famous for his *falsetas* (improvised interludes).

Carlos Montoya (1903–1993)   Son of Ramón; another popular flamenco guitarist.

Jimmy Page (1944)   British-born blues/rock guitarist famed for his work with Led Zeppelin.

Les Paul (b. Lester Polfus, 1915)   American guitarist and designer famous for inventing a solid-body electric guitar that bears his name and is manufactured by the Gibson Company.

Carl Perkins (1932–1997)   American-born country/rock guitarist.

Ida Presti (1924–1967)   Celebrated French classical guitarist who was half of the famous Presti/Lagoya duo.

Django Reinhardt (1910–1953)   Gypsy guitarist famous for his lightning-fast melodic playing in jazz styles.

Keith Richards (1943)   Lead guitarist with the Rolling Stones.

Jimmie Rodgers (b. James Charles Rodgers, 1897–1933)   American country/blues guitarist famous for his yodeling vocals.

Celedonio Romero (1918–1996)   Father and found of a famous quartet, The Royal Family of the Guitar.

Todd Rundgren (1948)   American pop-rock guitarist, vocalist, songwriter, and bandleader.

Carlos Santana (1947)   Mexican-born jazz-rock guitarist and bandleader.

Gaspar Sanz (c. 1600)   Spanish guitarist and publisher of a famed instruction book that first appeared in 1674.

Andrés Segovia (1893–1987)   Celebrated Spanish guitarist who performed throughout the world.

Paul Simon (1941)   American singer/songwriter and guitarist.

Fernando Sor (b. Joseph Fernando Macari Sors, 1778–1839)   Spanish guitarist whose works are still played today.

Bruce Springsteen (1949)   New Jersey–born rock guitarist, songwriter, and vocalist.

Francisco Tárrega (1852–1909)   Spanish guitarist who helped revive interest in the instrument in modern times.

James Taylor (1948)   American folk-rock guitarist.

Richard Thompson (1949)   British-born singer, songwriter, and guitarist famous for his work with Fairport Convention and his subsequent solo career.

Pete Townshend (1945)   British-born rock guitarist, songwriter, and vocalist famous for his work with the Who.

Merle Travis (1917–1983)   American country guitarist credited with developing "Travis" picking.

Ernest Tubb (1914–1984)   Texas-born country singer/songwriter who pioneered the use of the electric guitar in country music.

Ike Turner (b. Izear Turner, 1931)   Mississippi-born blues/rock guitarist and bandleader.

Eddie van Halen (1957)   American heavy-metal guitarist.

Stevie Ray Vaughan (1954–1990)   American blues guitarist.

Joe Walsh (1947)   American rock guitarist famed for his work with the James Gang and the Eagles.

Doc Watson (1923)   American country/folk guitarist known for his agile flatpicking.

Clarence White (1941–1973)   Country/rock/bluegrass guitarist.

Johnnny Winters (1944)   Texas-born blues guitarist.

Ron Wood (1947)   British rock guitarist famed for his work with the (Small) Faces and the Rolling Stones.

Neil Young (1945)   Canadian-born rock/blues/folk guitarist and songwriter famous for his solo work and his work with Buffalo Springfield, as well as his accomplishments in the band Crosby, Stills, Nash, and Young.

Frank Zappa (1940)   Eclectic American rock/jazz guitarist, composer, and vocalist, and leader of the group the Mothers of Invention.

Guitar Talk

Accent. To emphasize a specific note.

Accidental. A note that falls outside of the normal key signature of a work.

Acoustic guitar. The standard guitar, with no amplification.

Acoustic-electric guitars. Acoustic guitars with a built-in electric pickup for amplification.

Action. The height of the strings over the fingerboard.

Arch-top guitar. *See* jazz guitar.

Arpeggio. Literally, "harp-like"; playing the notes of a chord in succession.

Arrastre. *See* slide.

Axis. The angle at which you hold your picking hand. A 90-degree axis indicates the hand is held fully upright against the strings.

Bar. To place the left or fretting finger across a single fret to play a chord. Also called a full bar.

Bass guitar. A four-string guitar tuned like a standup bass but held like a guitar.

Beguine. A syncopated Latin dance with the emphasis on the first two upbeats.

Bend. A blues technique for varying the pitch by pulling the left-hand figure sideways.

Binding. Material used to hide the joints between the face and the sides of the guitar.

Boogie bass. A left-hand rhythm pattern derived from boogie-woogie piano styles, and commonly heard in rockabilly-style accompaniments.

Boom-chick strum. Alternating a bass note with a downward brush stroke across the three highest strings.

Bossa nova. Popular Latin dance of the sixties that combined jazz chords with a Latin rhythm.

Bridge. An attachment to the face of the guitar that is used to anchor the strings.

Bridge bone. A small piece of wood, plastic, or bone located on the bridge to separate the strings.

Cante chico. The more popular form of flamenco.

Cante hondo. The more serious form of flamenco.

Capo. A device that is placed around the neck of the guitar used to raise its pitch.

Carter-style accompaniment. An accompaniment style popularized by "Mother" Maybelle Carter, which consists of picking out the melody on the bass strings and brushing the high strings in between.

Case. A protective carrying unit designed to hold your guitar. Some cases are made of chipboard or paper, and others of cloth (called gigbags). The best are so-called hardshell cases of laminated wood or fiberglass.

Chord. A group of notes sounded simultaneously.

Chord block. A graphic representation of how to finger a chord on the guitar's fingerboard.

Chord chart. A diagram that shows the number of beats given to each chord.

Chord sequence or succession. A common pattern of chords used to accompany a specific style of music, such as a 12-bar blues. Also called a chord progression.

Chorus. A special effect available on electric guitars to add fullness to the sound.

Classical guitar. A guitar designed for playing the concert repertoire, usually smallish of body, strung with nylon strings, and having a slotted peg head.

Common time. 4/4 time.

Damp. To stop a string from vibrating.

Diminished seventh chord. A chord formed by stacking three minor thirds on top of any note. The interval between the tonic and the highest note is a diminished seventh.

Dominant chord. The chord based on the fifth note of the scale. Also called the five chord. When the seventh scale note is added, it is called the dominant seventh.

Dotted note. A note whose time is increased by half, indicated by placing a dot after the note. A dotted quarter note, for example, is held as long as a quarter note plus an eighth note.

Double sharp. A sign (x) that raises a note by two half steps; it can also be indicated by two sharp signs placed together (♯ ♯).

Downbeat. The primary or first accent in a measure.

Downstroke. To move the pick downward (toward the treble strings).

Dreadnought. A large-bottomed guitar developed by the Martin company and preferred by folk guitarists.

Eighth note. A note equal to half of the duration of a quarter note.

Electric guitar. An amplified instrument with a solid body having no inherent sound of its own without amplification.

Electronic tuner. A device that produces exact pitches used to tune a guitar.

Equivalent note. The same note sounded on a different string.

Face. The front or top of the guitar.

Falseta. An improvised melodic part placed at the end of each vocal line by flamenco guitarists.

Fan bracing. A system of internal braces often used on Spanish or classical guitars, in which the braces are placed in a fan pattern.

Fender guitar. An electric guitar developed by Leo Fender. Fender's two most famous models are the Telecaster and Stratocaster.

Fingerboard. The neck-like extension of the guitar, equipped with frets; the player presses on these frets to change the pitch of the strings. Also called fretboard.

Fingerpick. A small, metal extension placed on the fingers to help pick the strings.

First string. The highest-pitched string.

Flamenco. A popular Spanish folk-guitar style.

Flat. An indication to lower a note by a half step, denoted by the sign ♭.

Flat pick. A triangular pick held between the thumb and first finger, used to strum the guitar.

Folk guitar. An acoustic guitar strung with steel strings and a larger body size than the classical model.

Footstool. A low stool used by classical players to elevate one leg so that the guitar is positioned correctly against the player's lap.

Free stroke. Movement of the right or picking hand freely against the strings.

Fret. A small piece of steel inserted into the fingerboard that is used to set the pitch of the strings.

Full bar. *See* bar.

Fuzztone. An electronic, artificial distortion device added to the guitar.

Gauge. The width of a guitar string; heavier-gauge strings are harder to play.

Golpe. A rhythmic tap against the faceplate of the guitar, used in flamenco.

Guide finger. A fretting finger that is held just above the string, used as a method of guiding the hand up the neck.

Guitar synthesizer. An electronic or digital synthesizer shaped and played like a guitar.

Gut strings. *See* nylon strings.

Half bar. Placing the left or fretting finger across two to five strings at a single fret. *Compare* bar.

Half note. A note equaling two quarter notes, or two beats in common time.

Half step (half tone). The distance between one note and the next adjacent one.

Hammer-on. Dropping the left or fretting finger onto a string after picking it, to produce a second tone.

Harmonic. The partial tone that is created when a string is touched lightly at a specific point, known as a node.

Harmony. A pleasing combination of melody and accompanying chords.

Heel. The back of the neck where it joins the body of the guitar.

Hollow-body electric guitar. An acoustic guitar with a built-in electric pickup.

Independent voice. A separate melody line.

Jazz guitar. A larger-bodied guitar, often with an arched or carved top and back, and sometimes having f-shaped sound holes.

Key signature. Indication at the front of a staff showing which notes are to be sharped or flatted, and showing the specific key that a piece of music is written in.

Laminate. A thin wood veneer applied to a inexpensive base to make an instrument appear to be made of a better (and more expensive) wood; plywood.

Major chord or scale. Literally, "greater" as opposed to "lesser" (minor). The primary scale key for each tonic (starting note).

Major seventh chord. This chord is formed by raising the seventh note of the dominant seventh by a half step.

Measure. A unit of rhythm defined by the time signature.

Metronome. A mechanical device used to establish a regular beat.

Minor chord or scale. Literally "lesser"; the related key to the major, minor keys are usually thought to be sadder sounding.

Minor seventh. The minor triad with the addition of the seventh scale note.

Mixed rhythms. Measures that include a mixture of different time values, such as quarter notes, eighth notes, and sixteenth notes.

Movable chord. A chord that, when played in a different position, produces a different chord.

Music notation. A system of writing music down on paper using a music staff.

Natural sign. A symbol (♮) indicating that a note should be neither raised (sharpened) nor lowered (flattened).

Ninth chord. The dominant seventh chord, with the addition of the ninth scale note.

Nut. A small piece of plastic, bone, or wood placed at the bottom of the peg head to align the strings properly.

Nylon strings (or gut strings). The customary strings used for classical guitars. These strings have a soft tone and are made from nylon or animal gut.

Octave. Two notes having the same tone but pitched eight scale steps apart.

Pedalboard. A system of foot-operated pedals used by the electric guitarist to control special effects, such as chorus or wah-wah.

Peg head. A device located at the top of the guitar's neck, used to hold the tuning machines that tune the strings.

Picado. Picking of melody notes in flamenco.

Pickup. A transducer mounted in an electric guitar that converts string vibrations into electrical signals that can then be amplified.

P-I-M-A. The thumb *(p)*, index finger *(i)*, middle finger *(m)*, and annular ring finger *(a)*; designations used to specify the picking fingers of the right hand in classical music.

Pitch pipe. A small set of six pipes used to tune the guitar.

Portamento. Gliding from one note to another; the first and second notes are both picked. *Compare* slide.

Position. The placement of the fretting hand on the fingerboard; for example, anchoring the fretting hand at the fifth fret is known as "fifth position."

Pull-off. Removal of the left or fretting finger after a note is already sounded, to create a second tone.

Purfling. *See* binding.

Quarter note. The basic note value in 4/4 time, equaling one beat.

Rasgueado. Literally, "scraped"; rhythmic percussion-strumming in flamenco.

Relative minor. The minor chord formed from the sixth note of the major scale; for example, A minor is the relative minor to C major.

Relative tuning. Using one string as a reference, tuning all the others by fretting the required notes.

Rest. An indication that no notes are to be played for a specific length of time.

Rest stroke. The technique of picking the string whereby, after the pick strikes the desired string, it comes to rest on the string below it.

Rhythm. The basic organization of beats within a piece of music.

Rhythm of bulerías. A twelve-beat rhythm common in flamenco music.

Rosette. A fancy inlay around the sound hole.

Rumba. A syncopated Latin dance with the emphasis on the second half of the second beat.

Scale. A special relationship of whole and half steps.

Sharp. An indication to raise a note by a half step, denoted by the sign ♯.

Shuffle beat. A long-short accompaniment rhythm pattern.

Sixth chord. The major triad with the addition of the sixth scale note.

Slide. Moving the fretting finger from one fret to another, creating a sliding sound; also called *arrastre*. The second note is not sounded by the picking hand. *See also* portamento.

Slur. Moving from one note to another by using the fretting finger. *See* hammer-on and pull-off.

Solid body. *See* electric guitar.

Sound hole. Round, oval, or f-shaped sound holes are said to enhance the sound of the guitar.

Spanish guitar. A guitar similar to the classical variety, but usually made of cypress wood because of its more metallic sound.

Silk-and-steel strings. Midway between nylon and steel strings, these are made with a nylon core that is wound with metal.

Sixteenth note. A note equal to half the time value of an eighth note.

Sixth string. The lowest-sounding string.

Staff. In music notation, the five lines on which notes are placed. In guitar tablature, the six lines used to indicate the six strings.

Steel strings. Strings made from various types of metal; used for both acoustic and electric guitars.

Strap. For players who prefer to stand, a strap is used hang the instrument against the body, so the hands are free to play.

Subdominant chord. The chord based on the fourth-scale step; also called the four chord.

Syncopation. Melody notes that fall on the unstressed beats (offbeats).

TAB. Abbreviation placed in front of a line of music to indicate that it is tablature and not standard notation.

Tablature. A system of notation showing the position of the fingers on the guitar's fingerboard or neck.

Tango. A syncopated Latin dance with emphasis on the upbeat.

Tempo. The speed at which a piece is played.

Texture. The overall sound of an arrangement, including the number of notes played, how loudly or softly they are sounded, their relation to the vocal part, and so on.

Thumbpick. A small, metal pick attached to the thumb.

Tie. A mark used to indicate that two notes of the same pitch are to be played as one, and held for the duration of their combined time values.

Time signature. A symbol that takes the form of a fraction whose upper number indicates how many beats are in each measure, and whose lower number shows which type of note equals a beat.

Tonic. The first note of a scale from which it takes its name; for example, C is the tonic of the C major scale. It is also the name of the chord derived from the first scale note—in this case, the C-major chord (C-E-G).

Transposing. Moving a melody from one key to another.

Travis picking. A style of folk picking developed by guitarist Merle Travis. A regular bass is established with the thumb, and a syncopated melody is played against it.

Tremolo. Moving the pick rapidly up and down to make a wavering sound. *See also* vibrato.

Triplet. Three notes played in the time usually allotted to two; for example, three eighth notes linked together would equal a single beat in common (4/4) time.

Tuning fork. A fixed-pitch instrument used to tune a single note.

Tuning pegs. The gears or machines used to tune the strings.

12-bar blues. The most common blues chord accompaniment pattern.

12-string guitar. A large-bodied guitar with six pairs of strings, tuned in octaves.

Upbeat. The unaccented beat between the main beats.

Upstroke. Moving the pick upwards (toward the bass strings).

Vibrato. Bending a string rapidly with the fretting hand to make a wavering sound.

Vihuela. A sixteenth-century Spanish guitar, with six pairs of strings.

Wah-wah pedal. A special device that adds a "crying" effect to the electric guitar.

Waltz. A Viennese dance characterized by its 3/4 rhythm and heavily accented first beat.

Whole note. A note equaling two half notes, or four beats in common (4/4) time.

Whole step. Two half steps; the distance between a note and the second pitch above it in the common 12-tone scale, called a major second.

X-bracing. A system of internal bracing that makes a guitar strong enough to withstand steel strings; first used on Martin guitars.

Index

CD Track List

Working with Your CD

The CD that accompanies this book serves a dual purpose. First, it gives you the opportunity to hear the pieces that you will be studying played correctly in tempo. Second, and perhaps more important, it gives you the opportunity to play along as if playing a duet with a teacher, singer, or instrumentalist. Your parts are recorded on the right track, and the second parts, either teacher accompaniments or melodies for you to accompany, are on the left track. Thus you can learn your part playing with the right track, then play in duet with the left track. This interactivity presents some challenge and is an excellent way to learn when a live teacher is not available.

The track list enables you to coordinate your book and CD, and a helpful slogan to remember is "You're always on the right track."

CREDIT FOR CD

Instrumentalists: Edward Flower, Guitar
               Nellie W. Fink, Flute

Produced by Edward Flower and Nellie W. Fink.

Recording Engineer: Greg Steele of Derek Studios (Dalton, MA)